"**Growth or Bust!** is not only a book to be read, but studied. Faust's book reveals the need for the holistic approach...make it long-term and systemic with sustainable, continuous improvement led by the management team to move a company or organization forward deep into the future."

—Ford Taylor, turnaround CEO of several nine-figure apparel companies

"Faust has created a timely and pragmatic guide for achieving turnaround success, which has never been done before...any company will benefit from **Growth or Bust!**."

—Tim Caldwell, five-time turnaround CEO and founder of several start-ups

"Faust has identified for business owners the drivers of change and how to get their management teams thinking about innovation, strategy, and staying ahead of the pack. This isn't just a book, but a working reference guide to keep on your desk for frequent reference."

—William M. Custer, venture capitalist and CEO of Custer Capital, Inc.

"Mark's work with us and the principles in this book have been and will continue to be growing revenues and profitability. I highly recommend any leader to read **Growth or Bust!**!"

—Alan Hagie, president and CEO of Hagie Manufacturing

"We've seen these strategies facilitated into our company in our work with Echelon...this book gets very specific about the what and the how; great stuff...any leader who wants to grow their company will benefit from **Growth or Bust!**!"

—John Latham, CEO of Latham Seeds

"Mark's speeches on the topics in this book have been some of the most popular and results-oriented at our speakers' bureau. I know these principles work, because we used Mark at my first company, which grew rapidly and was sold in no small part to the principles in this book being applied through Mark's work.

—Joe Condit, CEO of CMG Speaking Bureau and
founder of several successful start-ups

"I've worked with Mark for more than 15 years and have successfully employed these principles throughout our engagement. I believe **Growth or Bust!** is an outstanding practical playbook for managers and sales professionals alike."

—Kevin Hughes, managing partner of Rhinestone Group,
top thought leader in commercial real estate,
and a past president at Colliers International

"I LOVE this book! Mark Faust shares his significant experience and unique insights in a can't-put-it-down style. **Growth or Bust!** is a must-read for everyone on your management team!"

—Dan Lincoln, president of the Cincinnati
Convention & Visitors Bureau

"**Growth or Bust!** is a must-read for your entire management team. I've had my team read it and we have gleaned many ideas that we have already implemented, and still more we will put into practice. We have already experienced significant growth because of the ideas in this book and our work with Echelon."

—Ton Van Der Veldon, president of
Enza Zaden North America

"Mark Faust takes us for a walk through the untapped and unseen where the real growth potentials and turnaround levers are most frequently found."

—Rick Hughes, president of the Kansas City Convention & Visitors Association

"Great book; these principles would work for even the most successful of companies. I've seen them increase profitability firsthand."

—Anthony W. Hobson, JD, V.P. Counsel, North American Properties

"While management may benefit from this book the most, sales and marketing need to study chapters 5 through 12 for strategies they can implement. This is a treasure trove of great ideas for growing your company. I've seen Mark implement these strategies at several companies and they consistently work."

—David Jeffery, turnaround VP of sales for three medical products companies, and former top trainer at J&J's Ethicon

"**Growth or Bust!** is a virtual owner's manual for any entrepreneur looking to grow or turn around their business. The strategies in this book link to 'executables' that can have an immediate impact."

—Jeff Beckham, CEO of Kingsgate Transportation, a "Most Trusted 3PL" and a Cincinnati Business of the Year

"Not another paradigm shift but a TURNAROUND strategy that achieves real business growth. This book incorporates the same principles that made Mark one of the best and most practical speakers to serve at our annual conferences. Use this book!"

—Greg Ruehle, president of the Independent Professional Seedsmen Association

"This book is a powerful, practical, thought-provoking series of great ideas you can use immediately in your business to get great results."

—Brian Tracy, author of Full Engagement

"Both in his interactions with the board and in this book, Mark puts forth solid advice that helps to accelerate growth."

—John Hagie, Chairman of the Board at Hagie Manufacturing

"Mark has gleaned insights on turnarounds from a wide variety of business leaders and put them into one source. Whether you're trying to increase sales in a Fortune 500 company or membership in a nonprofit association, you'll discover practical growth strategies any organization can benefit from."

—Leonard Hoops, president of the
Indianapolis Convention & Visitors Bureau

"Mark's ideas have been a great help to me in identifying areas to grow my company and provide the ways and means to make changes to help me get that job done. His new book mirrors the help that he has been to me and will be a good resource for any company and its managers."

—Kelly Keithly, Chairman & CEO of Keithly Williams, largest
supplier of seeds in the Southwest

"Any company should be able to glean dozens of growth strategies from this book. I'd recommend it to anyone in management, marketing, or sales."

—Herb Rackliff, GM at Hyatt, winner of the top GM and
hotel property awards

"Mark Faust's tactics and strategies for my business have been right on target, and very beneficial. His common-sense approach has been very insightful. This book nails it."

—Todd Bender, president of Bendershima.com and the world's number-one skeet shooter

"Mark's work and this book are sound principles anyone can apply. I've seen them have a multimillion-dollar impact on our company."

—Travis Stahlkamp, director of business development, Hagie Manufacturing

"This collection of growth strategies for business leaders is the most practical and specific toolkit for growth I've ever read. These are exactly the steps we need to grow business and our economy."

—Congressman Bob McEwen, speaker and author on economic growth

"This is a carefully written, practical analysis on how to grow an organization. It is relevant to any firm that has made the commitment to capture a greater share of its market. I salute the author, for this is an outstanding book."

—Lawrence Higdon, CEO of Higdon Group and founder of several profitable start-ups

"This is a great book! I was faced with the challenge of turning around the lack of mortgage production at a federally chartered credit union. Mark's counsel was invaluable. After following his strategy, production increased exponentially. His advice was spot on. This book gives a detailed plan on how to achieve the same kind of results for any business. I've never seen any other book get so specific as to the steps needed to facilitate a turnaround."

—Dennis Straw, turnaround CEO of Mortgage Brokerage Companies

GROWTH
OR
BUST!

Proven Turnaround Strategies
to Grow Your Business

GROWTH
OR
BUST!

GAME-CHANGING SECRETS FROM A
LEADING CORPORATE STRATEGIST

MARK FAUST

CAREER
PRESS

Pompton Plains, N.J.

GROWTH OR BUST!
EDITED AND TYPESET BY KARA KUMPEL
Cover design by Wes Youssi
Printed in the U.S.A.
Images on pages 35, 54, 70, 165, and 173 are courtesy of Studio Art Services.

To order this title, please call toll-free 1-800-CAREER-1 (NJ and Canada: 201-848-0310) to order using VISA or MasterCard, or for further information on books from Career Press.

The Career Press, Inc.
220 West Parkway, Unit 12
Pompton Plains, NJ 07444
www.careerpress.com

Library of Congress Cataloging-in-Publication Data

Faust, Mark.

    Growth or bust! : proven turnaround strategies to grow your business / by Mark Faust.

            p. cm.

    Includes index.

    ISBN 978-1-60163-162-6 -- ISBN 978-1-60163-664-5 (ebook) 1. Leadership 2. Strategic planning. 3. Consumer

    satisfaction. 4. Industrial management--Technological innovations. I. Title.

    HD57.7.F38 2011

    658.4'06--dc22

                                                                              2011003523

Dedication

To our modern-day heroes: the business leaders who have
enough guts—and humility—to admit that their customers,
both internal and external, are the source of their future
success...because the turnaround of a business and our
long-term economy depends on it.

Acknowledgments

Most any book like this is the result of a multitude of relationships. I would like to give acknowledgment to all those who have enabled me to write this book:

To every family member, friend, and client; to every author of each of the 50 to 70 books I aim to read each year—because we only grow through relationships, and it is the people we meet and the books we read that make us who we are.

To every colleague, all of my mentors, advisors, and professionals who help me in my business; to every CEO and turnaround expert who granted me interviews and shared their wisdom—especially John Pepper, chairman of Disney and former CEO and president of Proctor & Gamble, who turned them around during a turbulent time, for investing his time with me.

To the editors of my articles and books, for helping me with my malapropisms, split infinitives, solecisms, and general abuse of the King's English.

To Michael O'Rourke, the most engaging writer and dedicated soldier I've ever met. He represents those who put aside their own goals and dreams so that we may pursue ours. May we all do so with passion.

Contents

Objectives; Growth Objectives From the Bottom Up; Accelerate Growth Management by Turning Managers Into Strategic Growth Coaches; Prioritizing or Defining One Central Growth Objective

Foreword

Sandy Costa was president and COO of the S&P 500
Quintiles during their six-year growth from $90 million to
$1.6 billion and from 1,000 to 20,000 employees. There were
many successful acquisitions in that time—a feat in and of
itself—but more than 60 percent of that growth was organic.
Prior to joining Quintiles, Mr. Costa held the positions of
General Counsel and Senior Vice President Administration
with Glaxo, Inc., U.S. Area Counsel with Merrell Dow
Pharmaceuticals, and Food & Drug Counsel with Norwich
Eaton Pharmaceuticals. In addition to Chairman of the Board
at Labopharm, Mr. Costa currently serves as director
of Cytokinetics and Biovest I. Mr. Costa is an adjunct
professor in the clinical research program at the
Campbell University School of Pharmacy.

Whenever I speak on the attributes of great leaders, the first requirement I list is the ability to get things done. To some, that may appear as stating the obvious, but it's not. We really enjoy drafting vision and mission statements; it stimulates our creative juices, and we get to devise lofty goals and aspirations. But it's after we settle on a vision, it's after we agree on a way forward that the really difficult work begins. If a company is to succeed, you and everyone in your charge must come to work daily with an obsessive focus on bringing those aspirations to ground, on making a vision reality.

In my experience, there are lots of business books that are long on theory, but wanting on how to apply that theory. At last, a business book that actually shows us how to get things done!

I often told folks who worked with me that the *only* line on an income statement that we can't manage is the top line. In some ways that is true. When revenues are tallied at the end of a quarter, they stand as they are. But before that number is posted, there are a myriad of things that can be done to increase revenues. Mark Faust provides countless teachings on how to move an organization forward. Practices that have worked for Mark during his long and successful consulting career.

Mark first lays the groundwork of why things go wrong and then tells you how to fix the problems befalling an organization. When a company is not performing up to expectations, we often feel as if we are drowning in remedial ideas. In this book, we are given concise and ordered plans to remedy a myriad of lapses in the workings of a company, as well as how to deal with the most important constituent outside its walls—our customers.

Mark will help you inject a new sense of realism into your team. He helps you and your coworkers manifest a new reality—a reality that strategy must be process-driven. A reality that every member of your team must be concerned with the welfare of every coworker and every department. In Mark's words, seeking that reality is "...a key requirement for personal success and that of the whole." Another reality—can your company *truly* assess its performance and how it measures up against the competitors? For some, it may be a novel concept to learn firsthand how its customers view the competition, rather than relying on internal self-serving assessments of the enemy.

Are you confident that you have a realistic understanding of how your customers view your company and the services or products you provide? Your marketing and sales folks may be telling you that your existing relationships are healthy, as business continues to come through the door. But if a customer is becoming dissatisfied, would you know it? The fact is, customers seldom complain, believing that it's your job to figure out that the ship has sprung leaks. And they are right. If customers aren't pleased with the services or products your company provides, your first and only clue may be when they find another provider. Mark provides cogent advice on how to really understand your customers' view of your company, and, of equal importance, how they perceive your competitors!

Have you ever considered that lots of folks within an organization don't know how their company makes money? It's true. For some, increasing revenues and profits simply boils down to winning another slice of business—and that helps, but have they really considered the organic changes necessary to improve the sales process? Dale Carnegie taught us that in any negotiation the opposing party is fixated on only one question: "What's in it for me?" Have you considered whether your proposals have a crystal-clear answer to that question? Mark has; he understands that "Regardless of your success with proposals, you would probably do well to go through a proposal innovation effort." Then he shows you how. He explains why the most effective way to generate additional business is to focus on existing customers. Is that where your search for additional business begins?

Mark's business philosophy speaks to an inclusive work society. When a problem crops up, he believes in getting as many people as is practical involved in key decisions. This is an important teaching. Why? As a leader you don't need folks to *agree* with your decisions, you need them to *accept* your decisions. Give people a say in developing something and they will take ownership, even if the final product differs from what they recommended. Mark details how that process can be both successful and personally rewarding for all involved.

I have often said that business, when conducted ethically, is the world's greatest indoor sport. Although I am not one to use sport metaphors, it is important to be constantly reminded that every business sector is an intensely competitive arena. Knowing this, Mark places great attention on understanding the interaction between sales and marketing organizations. He demystifies the common barriers and cultural impediments that often exist between these departments and explains how to construct the mutually beneficial interactions essential for any organization to flourish.

A company's culture turns toxic when individuals expend their energies in trying to best the folks they should be working with, rather than using those energies to best the competition! Mark reminds us that at the end of the day the battle for business should take place outside the borders of a company. Coworkers in the most successful companies come to work each day with the mindset that their company is in a fight for its life. Those that populate success-driven companies know that there are people just like them who will spend every moment of the workday trying to beat the tar out of the competition. Mark will show you how to rekindle a healthy sense of competitiveness. It will not only lead to profits, but coming to work each day will also be a lot more fun!

In some ways, **Growth or Bust** is a cookbook. A very sophisticated cookbook containing countless recipes for success. When Mark speaks of the need to instill certain values and practices in an organization, he doesn't stop there—he details exactly how a leader can do so. We can customize the message, add our own personal spices and seasonings, but a thoughtful, pragmatic recipe created throughout decades of observation and practice is provided as a starting point.

Perhaps what I like most about this book is that buried in Mark's lessons is a respectful recognition that there is a dignity to work. Work is more than an exercise aimed at creating profits or providing wages so folks can acquire things. Mark understands that there are few personal endeavors as nurturing as a meaningful work experience. That there is little else we do that can enhance our self-esteem as much as being with a group of people pulling on the same oar toward a transformational goal. We are intensely social beings; it's how we are wired. And so it is that deep, lasting friendships are formed and bonds of profound respect established when a team of coworkers set out in times of adversity to create something of lasting value.

Dear Reader, Mark Faust is a kind and caring man who has dedicated his life's work to helping others. He genuinely believes that his teachings will help you succeed. So do I. Mark is a winner; pay attention to what is printed on the pages that follow and you shall be as well!

Santo J. Costa

Chairman of the Board, Labopharm Inc.

May 2011

Introduction

How much untapped potential lies within your business?

If all the stars were to align and you had every tool you needed, if you made every effort possible, and if innovations yet to be thought of were implemented, how much more do you think you and your team as a whole could realistically create in annual sales revenue? In the same context, what is the maximum that one individual could sell or create in annual revenue (say in sales or marketing efforts) three years from now? Why can't several people on your team be performing at that level right now?

I believe and have experienced that the vast majority of companies have the potential to dramatically accelerate growth. With aggressive innovation and effective strategic planning, three-year objectives can often become this year's reality. But companies achieve this not from efforts focused just on marketing or individual selling skills or productivity innovations for growth, but by focusing holistically throughout a company. If a concerted effort is made to accelerate growth from every angle possible, often significant growth is right around the corner. This book is a turn-around manifesto for top management and sales and marketing management. It will help you to see what you can implement directly as well as where you could foster new or accelerated growth in other parts of your organization.

Employees often feel powerless in influencing the direction of a business. Yet I've found that the vast majority of successful top executives favor getting the best ideas from the troops on the front lines. Whether it's a specific innovation unique to your organization or an idea from this book, you have an obligation to continually share and seek ideas that foster growth in a business. And if new ideas and innovation aren't welcome or are discouraged in your organization, then you may be working in a crumbling culture that you'd be better off leaving.

Many teams will benefit most by reading this book together, with various sections given priority to specific groups. The objective is to identify and implement as many growth-oriented ideas as possible in management processes, marketing, selling, and customer interaction.

Improving sales and profits has little to do with sales training, consulting, or other quick fixes. I've experienced that most salespeople and teams are already gifted with enough ideas and ability to foster significant increases in sales and profits, but they are often harnessed by procedures that limit productivity or approaches that constrain the level of idea exchange and customer engagement. Fostering new growth is more about innovation than marketing angles, sales productivity, or skills; growth is more about a culture of continuous improvement than marketing blitz; growth is more about possibility-thinking than fear-fostering quotas. Your job is to prioritize a few new steps and ideas that can be implemented in a reasonable time. To grow your business, you must become the facilitator of innovation and a growth revolution.

Don't Just Choose to Take a Step Forward, Choose to "Turnaround"

The Revolution Solution

These ideas are a revolution for business for several reasons:

1. The vast majority of what is propagated as business literature is soft leadership, marketing, or story-based drivel with little practical step-by-step direction on how to execute ideas and concepts.

2. The vast majority of books on management are focused
    on just one facet of management; whether it be aspects
    of strategy, innovation, or employee-management issues,
    the business books of our day look too much at just one
    aspect of improvement and ignore the holistic approach
    as well as the many specific steps that leaders actually
    need to take in order to foster accelerated growth or a
    turnaround.

Whether your company's growth rate is not what it could be or
its very existence is at risk, your leadership team would do well to
take the attitude of facilitating a turnaround. I have seen the best
results when the CEO or other top leader declared boldly across
the company that "We are about to embark on a turnaround!" Or,
"As well as we are doing right now, I know that, with the talent
and potential in this organization, we are capable of much greater
things; we need to have an attitude that we are embarking on
an innovation and growth revolution." This attitude of "growth
regardless of current success" is one aspect of **The Revolution
Solution**. A determining factor of any possible growth is a leader's
belief in what is possible for his or her organization.

The alternative to a turnaround or revolution mentality is,
"Let's tweak and improve a few things just enough that we don't
upset what's working but achieve some improved profitability."
Your team will see it as just another management flavor of the
month. Too often leaders who approach growth this way are only
looking at a couple of areas of improvement. For example, they
might look at how they could increase sales and decrease production costs. The result of taking this piecemeal approach to improvement is that there will most likely be pushback from the
one or two areas you've decided to improve. Production will say,
"What about sales?!" Or sales will resent that you are focusing on
them while marketing is slacking in coming up with the new tools
or the new leads they have been begging for.

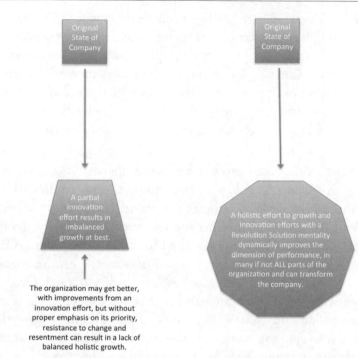

Your attitude, approach, and aim for areas in need of improvement must be holistic. Innovation should be fostered in all areas of any organization. Focusing on a few particular areas and omitting others, will breed bitterness and resentment and cause some to work to hinder success and direct blame."

The Benefits of a Turnaround Mindset

Whether your company is behind the eight ball with the clock ticking toward bankruptcy or there is little risk to your existence, I exhort your leadership to decide (and then communicate to the company) that "We are in turnaround mode." The statement adds a healthy amount of drama and emphasizes the significance of your new focus. Explain as well that dramatic cost-cutting is about to begin, but this does not mean people must be laid off.

Too often these types of slash-and-burn techniques are the tools of lazy, inept, uncreative, and unqualified leadership and consultants who are taking the easy way out of a challenging situation. Sadly, the idea of dramatically increasing profits through innovation and growth has become revolutionary rather than the norm. Now, what I am laying out here in this book *is* a bit of a revolution. It's a call to facilitate your own growth revolution. Jobs, families, and economies are counting on your success.

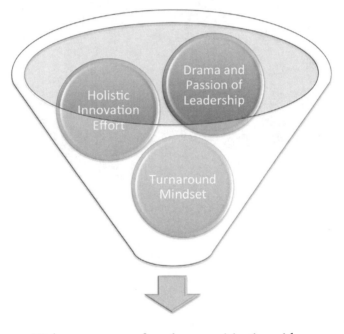

**Higher percentage of employee participation with
more emotional and creative intensity.**

Chapter 1
The Echeloned Innovation Process

Innovation is the root of all growth and every turnaround.

The two core functions of a business are innovation and marketing. The two are inextricably connected, and your team must understand what this means for your business and how they as team members must contribute. Innovation will be the fuel for turnaround and accelerated growth, while getting your team to truly understand marketing helps them to understand the priority of innovation and their role in it. They must understand that **marketing** is:

> The management process that profitably identifies, anticipates, and satisfies what the customer values.
>
> Seeing the business from the customer's point of view. This focus on what the customer values must permeate all areas of the enterprise.

After internalizing this definition, team members can then understand that they must have a balanced focus on the end customer—not just a focus on their internal customers.

Your team must also understand the definition of **innovation**, which is:

> Change that creates a new dimension of performance.

They must know that innovation doesn't only apply to product improvements, but to service and even internal process improvement as well. Most especially it needs to apply to all elements that effect the growth of revenue and profitability.

This chapter shows how to start a new emphasis on innovation where it can have an immediate return on investment, as well as how to implement an innovation process to improve sales and profits. At our client companies where we have facilitated the innovation process, the impact is consistently significant; seeing millions in potential profit improvement is not uncommon for small and mid-sized companies. Ensuring that your company is innovating in an ongoing process is guaranteed to produce significant rewards in your growth and bottom line.

7 Parts of Building an Innovation Culture

Innovation will grow your company faster than anything, and it must be holistic and touch every facet of your business. A corporate culture that is not fertile to cultivate such growth will quell profit-building innovation efforts. This is why you must often start with turning around your culture in order to make your team's hearts, minds, and hands work for an environment of growth-focused innovation.

1. Prioritize From the Top Down

The foundation for a culture of accelerated innovation is the titular leader's firm resolution and well-publicized commitment that *innovation is a top priority*. The top dog must consistently communicate this focus and motivate the team with it.

2. Clarify Your Innovation Values

Employees will want a values list to include things like respect and honesty, but the top leader needs to ensure that those values that are key to innovation's success are also included. Humility is a foundational value, as it requires everyone to admit that there could always be a better way, and that others may have better insight or answers. Open communication and safety in communicating problems are critical values, as people will clam up if an authority figure pounces on their suggestions for areas to improve.

To ensure that innovation at your company will be ongoing and not just a temporary spurt, you should build innovation not only into the company values, but also the growth objectives and the mission and vision as well.

3. Get All Hands on Deck

Because every facet of the business can be improved, every person must be committed to making regular efforts for improvement. Every person is exposed to at least a few areas of the business where they must be asked to think about what could be better. Management must require a minimum number of ideas to be turned in from every employee.

4. Initially Focus on Quantity vs. Quality

A key to success in innovation is generating the optimum quantity of ideas, as it is better to have created 1,000 new ideas (regardless of whether they are mediocre or impractical) than only a handful of excellent ideas in your initial efforts. Research consistently proves that a quantity of ideas will beget better-quality ideas in the end. This is because the multitude of ideas evolve and ultimately lead to the most valuable ideas for implementation.

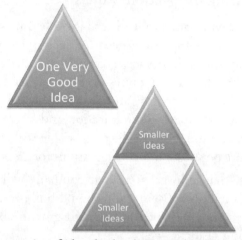

A quantity of ideas lead to better and bigger ideas.

5. Consistently Communicate Implementation and Successes

Getting everyone to begin looking for improvement opportunities and solutions for implementation changes the thinking and habits of the team. To continue the growth of such habits, employees must have a workplace environment with continuous feedback. Employees must regularly hear how their ideas and everyone's participation in innovation are improving their business with as many specific reports of improvements and implemented changes as possible.

6. Give Specific and Universal Rewards

Management may lament that it's everyone's job to keep an eye out for what can be improved, but the fact is that strategically recognized and incentivized good behaviors become repeated and habitual. Individuals who recommend ideas that have significant impact to profits should be given significant rewards. As the tide of innovation rises—a tide that is the result of a team contributing great efforts toward innovation—monetary and other rewards should be shared with the team. Innovation pays for itself and is self-perpetuating.

7. Make Innovation a Möbius Strip

Leading and managing the innovation process and culture takes work, and thus when times are good some may want to rest and ride out their competitive advantages. But innovation must be an ongoing process at sustainable levels. Avoid innovation efforts in spurts as this causes long-term employees to dub any new efforts the "management flavor of the day." The process must be more like the path of a Möbius strip: never-ending, consistent, and based on the single plane of an innovation-based, values-oriented culture.

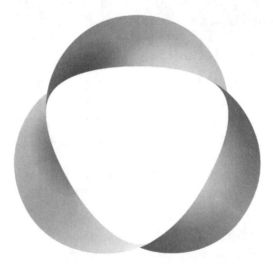

Like a Möbius loop, innovation efforts need to be ongoing and cover all facets of the organization.

7 Principles of Innovation

Your team will need to learn the principles of innovation and you will need to teach and reinforce them.

1. Innovation Is Holistic

No facet of the business is exempt from improvement, and no individual's role is exempt from participation in innovation. How clearly are these points understood and appreciated throughout your team?

To illustrate the point of how innovation needs to be holistically applied throughout the organization, you can ask your team to discuss the answers to these two questions:

1. What employees should not be included in the innovation process?
2. What part of the business isn't open for innovation and improvement?

2. Innovation Includes the Customer

The purpose of business is to get and keep a customer. You achieve that by knowing what the customer values and delivering with competitive advantage over the alternatives. And the surest way you can know what customers value is to ask them. Our clients are amazed at the innovations and improvements that customers will readily offer, but most businesses don't proactively involve the customer in this.

Ask your innovation leaders: Are we including the customer as much as possible in all the relevant areas of innovation? Ask the same of your customers. (We'll explore more on how to involve the customer in Chapter 6.)

3 & 4. Innovation Involves <u>Both</u> Organizational and Individual Opportunities for Contribution

When you are facilitating the idea-generation phase of the innovation process, there are two questions that should be regularly used:

1. What is one thing the *organization* can do to improve...?

2. What is one thing *you* can do to improve...?

It is easy for individuals to look around the organization and share what other divisions or the organization as a whole could do differently. You must challenge your team to first look at themselves and their own area of responsibility for innovations. In other words, *Ask not what your company can do to innovate, but what you can innovate for your company.*

Include your vendors in the idea-generation process and you may be shocked to see what they have to offer. Vendors will have a unique perspective and may be able to help you uncover improvements for your operation that are inspired by your competition. Ask your vendors, "Is there any idea or innovation in use at our competition that we could legally implement? What aren't we doing that we should be doing, based on your experience with our competition?" Vendor-appreciation "lunch and learns" with multiple vendors have been excellent forums for me to facilitate idea-generation sessions for our customers. I also have clients who have created and mandated for vendors, surveys that include innovation-oriented questions and idea-generation opportunities. These efforts yielded profit-building improvements that otherwise would never have been discovered.

In our Innovation 100 workshops, we are careful to ensure that the questions used in each individual's innovation plan have the right balance of organizational and individual focus. You must also remember to include efforts to encourage managers to do the following:

- ✓ Coach others in their units on implementing the innovation process, driving it completely throughout the organization.
- ✓ Work on how they can help build and improve the innovation culture.
- ✓ Reach out for cross-departmental participation.
- ✓ Reach up or out for resources and approval when needed—especially for innovations that will help to save a company.

5. Quantity Is Better than Quality...at First

The principle of getting a *quantity* of ideas in order to lead to the best *quality* of ideas is one of the most important principles of innovation. As has been proven in studies on business innovation, the quantity of ideas inspires more new and ultimately higher-quality ideas. It is often in the third generation or greater where a spin-off idea becomes the successful answer to a problem. Stories abound of how some of the greatest innovations and ideas came from an initial idea that was farcical, ludicrous, humorous, and/or impractical.

You want to look for opportunities to recognize or incentivize people who have given a great quantity of ideas. While being sensitive to avoiding burnout, you may want to set minimums on the quantity of ideas. Remember that ideas are organic, and like any living body, they need food; the food of good ideas is more ideas.

6. Direction Is More Important Than Dollars

It's not the amount of the dollars saved as much as the team's alignment and direction of improvement that will bring the most synergy—and, ultimately, the most dollars.

While you are involving all facets of your team in the innovation process, remember that many areas won't have the financial impact that others do. Be careful not to put too much emphasis on the dollar amount made or saved. Recognize and encourage even the smallest of improvements.

You may have heard the old dictum in business, "The 1-percent difference can make all the difference." There is a tremendous amount of truth in that statement. A 1-percent cost savings in many different areas, or a 1-percent increase in average sales pricing, can amount to a 15-percent or higher increase in profitability. So if it becomes de rigueur for members of your team to look for ways to improve things by even 1 percent, you may find a significant or even exponential increase in your profitability with the amalgamation of these many 1-percent improvements.

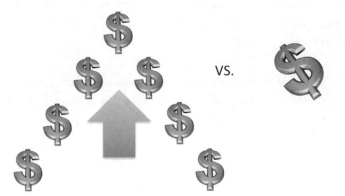

Emphasize the direction of any savings, not just the size of the dollars saved from only larger-impact ideas.

7. Innovation Is an Ongoing Process

A concerted innovation effort can potentially be rigorous and draining. You will need to be sensitive to how engaged your team can be during an intense campaign. But you must also never let minds stop being open to discovering opportunities for improvement. Innovation as a direction should be ongoing. You just need to be sensitive to the levels of focus and energy being put into it.

When you have a classic turnaround and people know they are fighting for both the life of the company and their jobs, focus can be sustained much longer, but you should continue to pay attention to your team's energy level. You can even just ask, "Are we pushing too hard on the innovation area? Do you or others need a rest?" Or, "On a scale of 1 to 10, where are we in the level of energy and amount of time we are putting into innovation, and where do we need to be?"

Keeping innovation ever alive and top of mind without causing burnout can be achieved by including small innovation efforts in any or all of your formal meetings. Many clients of ours take up the suggestion to make it a requirement for every meeting that every attendee bring a single new idea the company might be able to implement, as well as a single idea that he or she as an individual can implement.

In addition, to keep the innovation process ongoing, the official roles of your leadership team should include innovation responsibilities, and performance evaluations should include expectations and ratings on them.

7 Innovation Skills

1. Connecting the Unconnected

One innovation skill has to do with the ability to connect two unconnected issues for a new solution or dynamic. This is why you want diversity in your workplace and a disparity of backgrounds and experiences—they help foster creativity and ultimately more innovative solutions. A practice to encourage here is getting your team to look at solutions and innovations from outside your company, industry, and business.

2. Respectfully Challenging the Status Quo

Continually encourage your team to ask *Why, Why not*, and *What if* of many of the givens within your business. Great innovations come from someone asking a great question. I have seen some companies benefit by actually having a list of these questions that they will pull out when dealing with their top objectives, challenges, and constraints. Some good questions are:

✓ Why can't we do it this way?

✓ What would happen if...?

✓ Are there other industries or businesses that might have faced this same problem? How could we learn from them?

3. Flipping

Taking a position or issue and flipping it (or your conversation or consideration about it) to the opposite view is a common technique innovators use to change paradigms and discover new solutions. Playing devil's advocate or flipping an issue to the opposite possibility tends to create a synthesis and thus a new idea. If you were to have sales or marketing people regularly attempt to persuade you or others as to why a customer should buy from the competition, odds are you will all learn something, and perhaps innovate a new marketing or sales approach.

4. Embracing Constraints

Great questions create nonexistent constraints. For example, ask your team questions like, "If we weren't currently carrying this product or selling to this market or conducting business in this manner, would we even consider beginning to?" Or, "If we were legally prevented from selling to any of our existing customers, how would you make money next year?" A false constraint such as this challenges one's mind to think of alternatives that it otherwise would not. This is an excellent exercise to facilitate with a sales team to help them innovate ways to sell to more non-customers.

5. Studying Customers Like a Scientist

A common Japanese saying used in many businesses is *genchi genbutsu*, which means "going to the spot and seeing for yourself." The concept is to go to your customers as they are using your product or service and actually watching and intently studying them and their situation. (In Chapter 6 we will discuss how to interview them for untapped business and innovations.)

6. Experimenting

Perhaps you are already familiar with test marketing and the "A/B Testing" of alternate advertising campaigns to continuously improve your customer acquisition, but how much more experimentation could you do? When leaders talk about wanting to encourage their team members to be unafraid of failure and to learn from their mistakes, they expect their team members to engage in calculated risk-taking and continual experimentation to improve processes.

You should encourage your team to test and experiment more often for improvements they could implement. Consider holding lunch-and-learns where people share their experiments, lessons learned, failures, and of course successes.

7. Networking

In one company there hangs a sign in most every office. It reads:

> "The insights required to solve many of our most challenging problems come from **outside our industry** and scientific field. We must **aggressively and proudly incorporate** into our work, findings, and advances which were **not invented here**."

As a leader you must work to expel the NIH—"Not Invented Here"—syndrome and encourage your people to network widely inside and perhaps outside the industry. Some have said that changes only happen to people because of the books they've read and the people they've met. Finding places where best practices are shared, and where productive yet diverse relationships are built, will help to bring more innovation into your workplace.

The 7-Step Echelon Innovation Process

1. List Opportunities

What can be improved?

When I ask you for the top three constraints holding your company back from accelerating growth, you probably have no problem coming up with three very good answers. The same goes for when I ask you how you could be more effective in your role, and for some things that hold you back from being more effective. Those issues could be personal habits, lack of the proper tools, or environmental issues. The bottom line is, you are aware of individual and organizational innovation opportunities. Every one of your team members is just as aware of innovation opportunities. They all can contribute to the list of innovation opportunities. Your team's participation in the innovation process will build esprit de corps.

You must discern the best way to begin and continue to collect the opportunities for innovation. What we recommend in our innovation workshops is for individuals to list organizational and individual innovation opportunities they can start. This way they can immediately begin to personally facilitate the innovation process. Getting participants to focus on what they can change also helps to reduce finger-pointing and dissension.

2. Prioritize Opportunities

What has the highest ROI and likelihood for improvement?

Once an initial innovation opportunities list has been compiled, you will want to prioritize the list based on the key growth objectives of the organization. You may also need to base the prioritization on other factors, such as the likelihood of success and access to resources, but be careful not to assume that there are any unsolvable problems or unlikely opportunities. It amazes me how often we see "impossible" problems quickly resolved just by following through upon the innovation process. It was innovation around these "unsolvable" issues that ultimately led to significant competitive advantages for our clients, because often the competition had the same issue, and our clients were able to leap-frog them.

3. Invite Participation

Who are all the people that might be able to contribute ideas?

For each opportunity area you will need to determine who might be able to contribute ideas to it. Usually you will want to err on the side of being too inclusive rather than too restricted on whom you invite. I have seen transformative ideas for sales come from finance and revolutionary product developments on highly technical products come from sales. Some innovation opportunities should be open to the entire company, and areas that might seem very isolated often may benefit from including a few folks from outside the logical circle.

4. Gather Ideas

Gathering ideas can be as simple as collecting index cards or as complex as an online surveying solution. I have set up and used online tools that are built especially for our 7-step process, and I find that keeping the process "always-on" and available to approved participants is a great accelerant.

Simply sending out e-mails and compiling ideas will some-times work; other times you may see that setting aside part of a regularly scheduled meeting for the collecting of ideas is more effective. I often will set up innovation meetings solely for idea-collection and generation. The client and I may have the entire group working on just one opportunity area, or several groups breaking out to work on different opportunity areas. In the first phase of these meetings each person shares the ideas he or she has already collected or prepared. Then, after the group has seen the first version of the innovation list, a brainstorming phase takes place in which as many ideas as possible are added to the list.

The benefit of innovation meetings and brainstorming ses-sions is that there is a focused energy and attention that is synergistic. For some of your employees it may be hard to brainstorm on their own; participating in the group inspires people to be more creative and think more productively.

Online survey tools have several benefits: You can focus people through a very specific set of questions, and they can take their time reading and thinking over their ideas. You can also have a prioritization tool involved in the survey. I prefer to have a pass-word-protected database that not only stores the who, what, and when of opportunity areas and all ideas submitted, but also the ideas chosen to be implemented and an area for tracking follow-up and implementation.

5. Decide on Implementation

Finding the highest-quality ideas to solve problems or take advantage of growth opportunities is more likely with a larger list of possibilities. But then you have the essential (sometimes tedious) work of choosing either to immediately implement ideas or to research them first to see which ones may be more effective. For example, for marketing ideas aimed at getting prospects to respond to a mailing, you may want to test your best idea against the second-best with two test groups to see which idea actually draws the higher response. This can begin a continuous improvement process in such areas. You will find that many ideas will make for an obvious decision for implementation, but some may need to be parsed out for further research. The bottom line is, take as much action as possible, and implement furiously.

6. Communicate Success

Let people know how things are improving and how they played a part in the solution.

Innovation efforts can be looked at by some with a skeptical eye. People often abhor change, and you must be sensitive to the buy-in and support levels throughout your organization. Thus it will be critical for you to communicate success and reward it. Give regular and frequent feedback to your team about the implementation of their ideas and the benefits that you have realized. The more your team hears from you about the benefits and the more they experience them firsthand, the more support and involvement you will have throughout your organization.

7. Reward and Celebrate!

You will want to reward both individual and collective efforts. Certainly, giving monetary rewards commensurate with the financial impact of profitable ideas will rivet attention and spur ever-greater participation, but be careful. Some on your team may not have the exposure that others do to be a part of more significant profit improvements, and you need the entire team involved and committed to the process—otherwise, you may find sabotage as the result of resentment and jealousy. A lack of thorough support throughout the team could lead to the disintegration of your innovation process and ultimately your company.

It is a principle of good management to recognize good character qualities rather than performance. Everyone can display good character in their work—things like diligence, promptness, attentiveness, creativity, respect, and persistence. Although there are exceptions when you must recognize performance measures, such as in sales revenue generation, it is still best to tie these results and the impact of such great ideas to the character qualities and good habits that generated them. If you don't do this people may become resentful of recognition only going to performance and results, thinking, "I was part of helping on that project," or, "People have no idea how hard I work and how much less he works, and yet *he* is getting recognition for results of which he is lucky to be a part!" The fact is, in your business it takes the whole team to succeed, not just your quarterbacks and running backs.

To recognize effort and show appreciation for every idea some companies literally give a crisp new one-dollar bill for every idea card filled out and turned in. They also give $10 to those submitting exceptional ideas. Others recognize those submitting the most ideas with public verbal praise. You should innovate creative forms of recognition that you know will be of value to your teammates.

As you find times to regularly celebrate your team's participation in the process and implementation of ideas, try to do so in the most inclusive of manner—don't be stingy with gifts or incentives. I know of one company that was saved from bankruptcy by sharing a percentage of the savings realized by implemented ideas: A part went to the idea generator and a part went to the entire employee base. Everybody won. The employee base was focused on finding every possible innovation opportunity that could add to the bottom line. There was a true emotional ownership in not only the process but the fate of the company as well.

7 Rules for a Productive Idea-Formation Session

1. Embrace Change

A great leader gets his or her team to see change as fuel. Accelerated growth and turnaround can only come from positive change. Because people tend to support that which they help create, the more they are part of the innovation process the more they will embrace the change. However, you may want to avoid the term *change* in broad situations. People in general react negatively to the word, so *innovation* should be used in its place. But regardless of the moniker, the concept must be embraced.

2. Understand That There Are No Bad Ideas

This might be the most important yet least implemented rule of innovation and brainstorming. You must ensure that all participants accept all ideas. Guard carefully against your team blurting out harsh judgments against any idea. The remark "That's stupid!" could be the most poisonous phrase to your team's successful brainstorming. You must stamp out any such abusive judgment against ideas. The fact is, frequently it is the humorous, "stupid," impractical, or even impossible idea that is the impetus for a future idea that becomes the perfect solution.

3. Set Aside Titles, Status, and Position

In a brainstorming session, you must make employees from all levels of the company feel equal in the process. Make a symbolic gesture that there is no status or position around the brainstorming table. You must always be careful to choose good facilitators that will not break this rule themselves.

4. Postpone Discernment

At some point ideas will be sifted and prioritized, but in the idea-formation stage, you as the facilitator must postpone all judgment on any ideas. It is better to avoid having people even praise ideas in the brainstorming process. Unless you ensure every idea or effort to share an idea is praised, don't praise any idea at all. People will notice if few or none of their ideas were praised while others were.

5. Kill Idea Killers

Many people have a natural psychological proclivity to blurt out judgments, comments, or even looks that kill ideas. Almost every team has a person who constantly looks at why things won't work and immediately blurts out such thoughts. When you are facilitating brainstorming, you must be quick to kill idea-killing behaviors, and, if necessary, exclude people who can't control this habit. Perhaps the "judges" will serve excellently in the evaluation phase of the innovation process, but their harsh behaviors are verboten in all brainstorming.

6. Require Participation

Brainstorming sessions also require the facilitator to ensure that everyone participates. Often quiet people have a unique perspective. Diversity in the brainstorming team is extremely valuable, and to fully leverage the diversity of your team, you'll need to ensure everyone positively declares their point of view.

7. Say "Yes, and..."

Just after "that's stupid" would come "no" and "but" as some of the most dangerous words to productive brainstorming. You must get your team into the habit of listening to new ideas and literally saying "Yes, and..." as the perfect segue to another idea evolution. The phrase "Yes, and..." not only gives an appropriate affirmation and acknowledgment to the previous brainstormer, but it also builds on the idea, rather than contradicting and/or damaging it.

Leading the Echelon Innovation Process

Usually it is ideal to have one person become the CIO—Chief Innovation Officer. I feel most comfortable when it is the company president or other titular leader. Just as quality control efforts demand the top leader's buy-in, it is critical that the top leader is openly and consistently supportive of, if not actually leading this mission-critical aspect of the turnaround or growth acceleration effort.

You will also benefit from having an innovation team that is supporting the CIO. In many companies I find it productive to rotate participation on that team. It's a great cross-training and leadership-development opportunity, but perhaps more importantly it helps to ensure a fresh approach and diversity in the ongoing process. It also improves the likelihood of follow-up on details if that is not within the means of the CIO.

You will base where you need to begin on what is most in need of turnaround or improvement. Frequently in a flailing company, the culture is unhealthy especially in regard to being open to innovation and unafraid of change. To overcome this, leadership will need to be evangelistic, and unafraid to call out the root issues causing the pushback.

As overwhelming as your situation may be, you can take solace in the simplicity of the 7-Step Innovation Process, and feel comfortable in putting most of your focus there if that is all that you feel you can handle. Just clarify the chief objectives, such as to improve profits (getting out of the red if need be!) or just to accelerate growth, and walk through the seven steps:

1. List opportunities.

2. Prioritize opportunities.

3. Invite participation.

4. Gather ideas.

5. Decide on implementation.

6. Communicate success.

7. Reward and celebrate.

With diligence and humility in the process, you should have much to celebrate in due course.

Chapter 2
The Echeloned Strategy Process

It seems that 80 percent of the leaders of small to mid-sized companies feel that they have a well-defined and complete strategy all mapped out and effectively being followed through. But the reality I see after auditing many of these plans and supposed strategic processes is that the vast majority of companies *don't* have a fleshed-out strategy and are missing several key elements, such as decisions on direction, essential areas of objectives, and, most importantly, steps that make a strategy a process. Most companies could significantly build up, rev up, and more effectively follow through on an intensified growth-focused strategy. Ensure that there is a regular, quarterly walk-through of your strategy and constantly look for the areas where you can punch up your strategy with more aggressive and growth-oriented steps. Also consider an annual or even semi-annual complete audit of your strategy, objectives, and progress by an outside third party. Executives have personal coaches; why shouldn't companies have strategic growth coaches?

You want to go beyond your past interpretations and expressions of the strategic planning pyramid for Vision, Mission, Values, and Roles in this chapter. The current forms of these aspects in your existing strategy may be limiting, so begin an audit, and facilitate a "souping up" of these areas. Here are some methodologies for doing just that.

The 7 facets of an echeloned strategy process.

How to Construct a Vision of Significant Growth

Does your business have a compelling vision of growth that inspires your team? In our consulting, I've seen teams and individuals reach three-year revenue objectives, doubling and even tripling the rate of revenues in just 100 days, because of having a crystal-clear three-year target vision and initiating significant amounts of innovation. I encourage you to have both leadership and sales producers create "Blue Sky" objectives that focus on what is possible—not just probable—in a growth pattern over at least a three-year period. When possibility objectives have been set and are continuously strategized upon, revenues inevitably increase because of the innovations that are discovered and implemented.

In the classic sense, a vision and its structure are quite flexible. A vision statement can be a five-page document of an owner's or leader's long-term desires, hopes, and dreams for a company, or a 10-word outcome-focused description of what an organization hopes to achieve in its market or in the world. Some companies have 100-, 50-, or 10-year vision statements. Some century-old companies that created 100-year vision statements have realized exactly what they intended. Other companies, especially those in survival turnaround mode, may have visions that are only looking out several months or quarters due to significant constraints and survivability issues. Often companies are in need of a turnaround because they never had a compelling vision, or even had a vision at all.

Top leadership usually shapes the vision statement, but it can also be a collective effort. For your purpose of turning around a company or forging ahead into an accelerated growth mode, I strongly suggest that you reshape your vision to be acutely angled toward aggressive growth, with specific detail about what you aim to realize. Just as I challenge every leader we work with, I challenge you to think about the answer to this question: If all the stars were to align, and your organization were to accomplish all that it possibly could accomplish in the next three years [or what you think the appropriate vision timeline might be], what are the most optimistic outcomes you can imagine your organization achieving? I like the three-year timeline because it's readily imaginable to most people. As one client quipped, "It's just the year after the year after next."

On the one hand, you need to balance any vision, goal, or target with a certain amount of realism so as not to lose the buy-in of your team. You should research, report, and discuss with your leadership team what past growth patterns have looked like for some of the most successful companies in your industry or of a similar nature or structure. This research can give incontrovertible proof as to what is possible, and it shouldn't be a limiting factor. You must emphasize with your team that fantastic future growth rates are based on innovations and changes that you have yet to discover or implement. So I challenge you to push the envelope, and create a vision that is both believable and highly optimistic.

Perhaps the greatest limiting factor in the growth of a business is the boundary of the team's thoughts. Myriad stories are available of great achievements based on visions that in some elicited mockery but in others inspired thoughts of faith and hope of what was possible. As a leader you must realize that your thoughts may be the single greatest constraining factor in the growth of your business. As a leader, your casting of a limiting vision may be the most limiting factor for your company. Far better for you to err on the side of aiming too high and too great in your hopes. If you have any doubt about the optimism and the appropriate stretch of your vision, you need to call in for an outside party's confidential advice.

There have been some presidents of our client companies who were about to cast a vision but held off on sharing it, and either listened to the team about what they thought was the fuller potential or just raised the bar from their original vision's target based on our exhortation. In most cases like this, a much greater achievement was realized. In other words, momentous growth in a company occurred, based on one single and relatively small change in the hope of the vision. A vision is as powerful in changing the course and achievement of a company as the relatively small rudder of a ship or a strand of DNA.

Ask yourself every quarter if there is any needless limitation in any aspect of your vision.

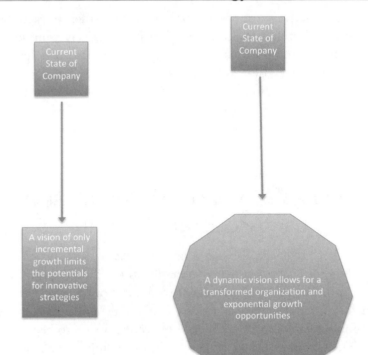

Communicating the Growth or Turnaround Vision

A vision kept secret is as worthless as no vision at all. Visions must be shared and discussed often, all throughout the organization. A great vision is a defensible competitive advantage that cannot be taken away from your company, so proclaim it boldly and often.

Your team may be languishing because they are unclear as to what the vision is or they may be uninspired by the long-term direction of your business. Their faith and motivation is built when they feel a sense of direction and greater purpose. Some leaders instinctively know what path to take in order to reach the business's vision and goals, but they aren't effectively communicating the vision and thus are limiting the speed and potential of achieving that vision. One of your top responsibilities is to communicate and discuss the vision. This responsibility isn't just for the titular leader, but anyone who is part of leadership. This is why it is critical for you to ensure that adequate buy-in to the vision is happening within the leadership team.

How a Clear and Focused Mission can Accelerate Growth

A short, concise mission that captures what you do for what kind of customers, with an emphasis on the significant return, profit, or growth you deliver to the customer, can become transformational in focusing sales, marketing, and other efforts throughout your company. The clearer your mission to help your customers grow, the more synergy it has in helping to accelerate growth for your own company. The following is a checklist of ideal features to have in a growth-oriented mission and the steps you can take to build it out. You can have your team answer "yes/absolutely," "no/not at all," or "somewhat" to these questions as a way to go through the process of refining your mission together.

✓ **Does your mission show how you foster growth for the customer?** The power of an excellent mission is that it focuses and inspires both employees and customers, thus impacting your company's growth. Does your mission inspire growth? Does it reference growth at all? Do you even have a true mission statement?

✓ **Does it inspire the team's commitment?** The mission should inspire; it is what you want your organization to be known for. Does it merely position your company as a provider of products, or does it position your company as a partner in the customer's success?

✓ **Does it define why you do what you do, and why your organization exists?** There are unique, powerful, and relevant reasons you are in the business you are in. Does your mission convey your competitive advantage or uniqueness? Too often the small company forgets the strength it has against its larger competitors. Are you just a local provider of your customers' needs, or are you a family-owned independent that can choose multinational providers' products based on what will make their business more money (as opposed to just selling a product because you manufacture it)?

✓ **Does your mission provide your team direction for doing the right things?** The old adage "In essentials, unity; in actions, freedom; in all things, trust" is in great need of emphasis with many businesses today. Your mission should help to direct action within your team. Ideally it should empower them to make more grassroots decisions and better serve the customer. Are you a company striving for quality service (as they all say) or a company that "aims to get customers to associate your brand with the absolute best service in the market" (to paraphrase a top-rated online retailer's mission)?

✓ **Does your mission address your opportunities for growth?** What is your potential in your market? What is the potential of your team, given your products and services? If you are aiming to be the number-one local provider of your services, or to innovate the best solutions for achieving goals never before set, then let it be known.

✓ **Does your mission match your competence?**

✓ **Does it say for what your company wants to be known or remembered for?** When you've helped a customer reach an important goal, is what they would say to their neighbor included in your mission statement.

✓ **Is it concise and sharply focused?** Is it clear, cogent, and easily understood? It should fit on a T-shirt—perhaps you should print up some "Mission Tees." Can your team and customer remember your mission, and is it catchy enough to make an impression? We've seen companies imprint their mission on shirts, stationery, and playing cards. When the benefit of what you do is clearly and concisely stated, positive branding occurs more frequently.

✓ **Should the mission be revisited?** If so, what changes should be considered?

Gather your team's answers and determine which aspects of your mission need refinement. Create a new version, and then conduct the self-assessment process on that, until a healthy version immerges.

How to Create and Reinforce a Set of Growth-Oriented Values and Commitments

You can trace the vast majority of all conflict within a team back to the lack of clarification on healthy, agreed-upon values, and/or a lack of reinforcement of those values. You can also trace a team's lack of follow-through on the strategy of a company, back to the lack of values reinforcing the strategic growth priorities.

Many companies have an old set of value statements, written by a founder or previous management team. These values might hang on the wall or be pasted into collateral. Unless they are vigorously reinforced they will wither and die and actually become the antithesis of their intent. Whether these old values speak of the priority of the customer and providing service or of treating others with respect, or even of being innovative, there are a few steps any management team can take to make this essential element of strategy more impactful and fuel accelerated growth.

Do you have conflict in your workplace, or is growth not as fast as it could be? What is the cost of conflict on productivity and effectiveness? Is there a lack of focus on priorities for accelerating growth and innovation, or a lack of enough attention on the customer? Aligning your company values to the direction you want to be going can make the difference in all of these areas.

To make values work as a tool for improving teamwork and reducing conflict, start by having your team answer a few key questions each year. This can be facilitated in an all-hands-on-deck exercise or in divisions (in the latter case the results need to be fed back to the entire team after all have participated).

The initial key questions are:

1. How do employees and customers want to be treated in the workplace?

2. What is important to us as an organization?

3. How will we deal with it when someone doesn't live up to our values?

Because people tend to support that which they help to create, everyone should have input into these answers.

To supercharge the values in an organization, and transform them into strategic, growth-oriented values, we also need to ask teams two other questions:

1. How should we conduct our work, both with each other and customers to optimize growth?

2. What kind of environment do we need to foster in our company, in our work, and in our relationships in order to maximize joy in the workplace, as well as the growth rate, profitability, and stability of this company?

Have every employee openly discuss the top traits, qualities, ways, habits, environments, and attitudes—in a word, *values*—that are needed to live and work by, and list this out. The list will usually have several dozen potential values. Then ask each individual to privately list out the top six of those values that he or she feels are the highest priority and that will most accelerate growth and improve satisfaction, happiness, and profitability in the workplace. Next, have employees team up in twos and agree on a top six values together. Then repeat the same process in teams of four, then eight, and so on, until the entire team has come up with their top six to 10 values that will create the optimum environment.

As facilitators, my company will then conduct a similar process around the question, "How will we deal with it when one of us doesn't live up to our value statements?" This is a much tougher but more important question, and key to ensuring that the values become the reality.

Depending on time, either the group or a committee could work on also building working definitions of each value, and perhaps give examples. Then, often my clients will have the final document printed on a poster and ceremoniously signed by the entire team. Leadership should regularly and publically recognize employees as good examples of walking out the values.

There may be strategically important values that only top management would recognize as a priority, so you will need to ensure that issues like the innovation in emerging businesses, new technologies, or the involvement of the customer are worked into the values as appropriate. The benefit of involving the whole team in this process is that it is a great team-building and communication exercise, but management must insure that all of the right values have been prioritized into the list and are adequately propagated and reinforced.

Most team-building exercises such as rope courses and falling backwards into your coworkers' arms are a waste of time when compared to having the team create growth-oriented values and strategic objectives that will work to accelerate growth. These exercises will also help to "Create Emotional Ownership"—the "C.E.O." of your growth- oriented culture. We've seen the values-clarification process be a key part in greatly increasing the growth rate and size of companies while making for a much happier workplace. This process can be transformational to cultures in need of a boost or turnaround. Revisit your values regularly and reinforce them both with accountability efforts and recognition of your exemplars.

The Read & Rip Method

People tend to support that which they help to create.

A great method to synthesize a group's contributions to the creation of a vision, a mission, values, and objectives is to use the Read & Rip method. It works this way: Assemble a small enough group that you can read their remarks aloud or post them in short order, such that they can read or hear and internalize each other's input rather quickly. With each phase of refining an issue you will ask the assembled group to write out their ideas or versions of the discussed issue (for example, the ideal mission statement or the ideal objectives for improving communications within your company).

Then you as the facilitator collect the ideas and read them aloud, or post them on a slide or flip chart. Each attendee's version is read through, and then, in dramatic flair you rip up the flip charts or whatever and say; "Okay, you have heard the group's thoughts on the ideal version of this issue; now, taking in the best of what you have heard, write out a newer, more inspired idea." You as the facilitator read and perhaps even rip again until you feel that a true synthesis has occurred among your participants.

This is a powerful team-building and synthesizing tool. Regardless of the size of the company—even with teams of thousands—I have used the tactic with great success in getting the team to feel that they have truly contributed to the output of whatever strategic issue has been addressed. And because people tend to support that which they help to create, this is one of the most effective methods to meld a team into one spirit and direction. Alignment and echeloning will occur with the frequent use of the Read & Rip method.

The Echeloned Role Exercise

Optimize the roles of your leadership team in order to optimize growth.

Rarely do executives, management, and knowledge workers leverage their talents as effectively as they could in the work environment. Here is a simple process you can regularly walk your leadership and teams through that will help them to spend more time doing the work that will accelerate growth and/or turn around your company.

One facet of the definition of management is leveraging the strengths of individuals and resources while minimizing the impact of their weaknesses. If you keep that definition in mind and consider the fact that most people know what they need to do in order to become more effective in their role, then you'll see that your task becomes to facilitate regular discussion on what it will take for your team members to do more of what they do well, and thus deliver a higher ROI and acceleration of growth. For all that, one of the most important management questions is, "What should we *stop* doing?" The following two role-clarification exercises will help your team to do less of what is holding them up from focusing on the growth objectives.

In more than 20 years of facilitating the following exercise, my experience has been that most people will be very accurate and honest in answering the following questions. But you must ensure that this exercise is conducted in a safe environment. At the end of this section I'll offer a few ideas that help to open the doors of communication. These questions follow a strategic pattern so as to engender a healthy dialogue among your team about role development and focus. Have your team members answer them in order.

1. My professional skill *strengths* as they apply to being a part of this team are:

2. My professional skill *weaknesses* as they apply to being a part of this team are:

3. The *strengths* of my personality that affect my roles in this team are:

4. The *weaknesses* of my personality that put a drag on the effectiveness of my roles on this team are:

5. The activities I *most* want to be doing on a regular basis for this team are:

6. The work activities I *least* want to be doing on a regular basis, yet might be normally required from me in my position on this team are:

7. The current definition of my role and responsibilities on this team is:

8. The changes I would like to see in my role and responsibilities on this team (or, what I would like to see my new role and responsibilities become in the near future in order for me to most help accelerate growth) are:

The presenter of those eight points will then be under a ban of silence, and each member of the participating team will give feedback on the following:

1. What I see to be your key strengths and what I recommend you do more of or focus more intently on.

2. What I or my team can do to better support you in your role or in the evolution of your role.

3. Things you could reduce or eliminate to free up time for your priority focus areas.

What I find fascinating in using this questioning strategy is that, most of the time, participants are surprisingly accurate and honest about their weaknesses and priorities.

I recommend that the highest-ranking leader go first in the exercise. His or her honesty will inspire the others to feel safe in opening up about their weaknesses as well. Also, the first to go can set the example of being receptive and silent during the feedback phase.

Maintaining Focus With the Semi-Annual Role Focus 12 Letter

An excellent best practice that can help to keep your management team focused on the right areas and help to resolve misunderstandings about their role and focus is the semi-annual use of the **Role Focus 12**.

The process requires each subordinate to write a Role Focus 12 letter to his or her manager, which answers the following 12 questions.

1. What are the top objectives of my direct manager's role?

2. What are the top objectives of my own role?

3. What are the performance standards that are being applied to me?

4. What are the major constraints/obstacles in my unit?

5. What are the things the company does that most help me?

6. What are the things my superior does that most help me?

7. What are the things my company does that most hinder me?

8. What are the things my superior does that most hinder me?

9. In the last six months the successes of my focus have been...

10. In the last six months the areas in which I wish I had done better were...

11. What accomplishments, projects, or deliverables do I propose to have done in the next year to reach the above objectives?

12. What are the activities on which I most need to focus in order to accelerate my progress toward these objectives?

Whereas a healthy company working toward an accelerated growth mode might only require the Role Focus 12 to be exchanged every six months, companies in a live-or-die turnaround may benefit from completing it more frequently, as roles and objectives may be changing at a faster-than-normal pace.

Facilitating and Building Your Growth Pyramid

With the tools in this chapter you will be able to facilitate the building of a more growth-oriented set of mission, vision, values, and roles statements. As we will discuss further in Chapter 4, all of these will need regular review as part of an ongoing process. This will ensure that your team is on the same page and that every aspect of the strategic growth pyramid is as aggressive as it can be in its focus on turnaround and/or growth.

Chapter 3
Echeloned Growth Objectives

The 7 Essential Areas of Objectives

Rarely do mid-sized businesses have clearly defined innovation and marketing objectives—let alone in all seven areas. The following seven areas are "essential" because every organization must set objectives for each of them, or risk seriously limiting their growth potential. In turnaround or accelerated-growth mode, you should look at each area from the standpoint of what will accelerate growth to the maximum extent without undue risk. Most of your objectives can be skewed toward an intensified focus on growth, which will have a positive impact on your results.

You must have your team go through an objective-clarification exercise for all of these areas. This does not need to happen in one fell swoop; it will be a process, but I usually find that at least a skeleton of most of these areas can be begun rather quickly, and refinement and alignment can be done in time. You will want to have a monthly tracking and a quarterly recalibration of your key objectives. This alignment process will help to focus daily activity and lead to successful improvements in your growth and profitability.

Ask yourself and your teams all of the many questions in the seven areas that follow in order to fully qualify your objectives and reach your growth goals.

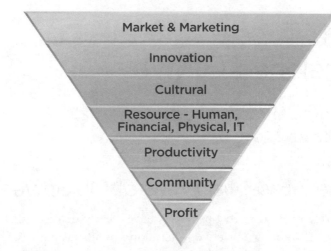

The 7 essential areas of objectives.

1. Market & Marketing Objectives

Market-related objectives should only be set after you have asked these two questions first:

1. What is your decision on concentration? What is your competitive advantage, and in what areas of the market can you be most successful?

2. What is your decision on your ideal market standing? There can be great dangers to having an 85 percent market share, just as having too small of a market share could be proof of gross ineffectiveness and lead to great vulnerability. It is better for you to have 50 percent of 250 than 85 percent of 100. Companies that are near monopoly face significant growth pressures and usually cannot effectively innovate. Choosing the most market share is not the objective; choosing the *optimal* market share is your objective. You must determine what is optimal.

Only then can you ask questions like these:

- ✓ What is your business, and what should it be?
- ✓ What is the result that customers buy from you, or what is the job they want accomplished?
- ✓ What areas might you not be adequately serving?
- ✓ What businesses, products, or practices, if you weren't in them today, would you still choose to get into? Which ones would you not enter, and thus, what markets might you need to exit, or what practices might you need to abandon?
- ✓ What new products and services for existing markets does the customer value, and how should you prioritize your actions for preparing delivery of them?
- ✓ How do you prioritize potential new markets, and what are the triggers that signal that you should enter them?
- ✓ What are all of the potential distribution channels you could employ? What are the advantages of each, and where might you consider changing your distributive organization?
- ✓ What is your customers' perception of your service, and how do you compare to their alternatives? What is the optimal service standard and performance you need to aim for, and how do you best leverage this strategic choice in the marketplace?

2. Innovation and Change–Related Objectives

What should your business be? Considering your competitive positioning (advantages, equalities, and weaknesses) as well as your resources, what should your business become?

What innovation do you need to foster in:

✓ **Product:** Products or services.

✓ **Social:** Your marketplace.

✓ **Management:** Skills and activities needed to make products or services; your approaches to managing and running your business.

As discussed in Chapter 1, the challenge is to prioritize the areas in which you will most benefit by innovating. You may realize millions in savings through excellent innovations in management and cost containment, but you may uncover *billions* in a new market with either product or market innovations. You will need to have a constant strategic balance of your team's time and resources.

3. Cultural Objectives

What are the strengths and weaknesses of your culture, and what do you need it to become in order to be more competitive? What is the ideal culture for optimized retention, productivity, and employee happiness?

4. Resource Objectives

What resources will you need in order to optimally perform and accomplish your mission? Think about the following types of organizational resources:

✓ **Human resources.** What do your jobs have to offer to attract and easily retain the kind of people you want and need? What talent is available on the job market? What do you have to do to attract and retain the right talent?

✓ **Financial resources.** What does the level of investment in your business need to be, in the form of bank loans, long-term debts, or equity, to attract and hold the capital resources you will need?

✓ **Physical resources.**

✓ **Information technology resources.** What physical or
IT resources do you need to cover the business's antici-
pated needs, structure, and direction and plans?

5. Productivity

What are the best yardsticks for comparing the management
of the various units within your enterprise? What are the productivity opportunities that, if improved, would most accelerate the
growth of your business?

It is important to note that regarding your physical resources,
human resources, financial resources, and IT resources if too much
of any one resource is used to make one "productive," then productivity has actually decreased. There must be a balance among
the resources of a business. Productivity objectives require you to
be in check as to whether you are getting all that you should be
out of your human, financial, physical, and IT resources.

6. Community and Social Responsibility

Your business is a creature of a society and an economy. How
can you as an enterprise nurture your society and economy, both
of which can continue to feed you—or put you out of business
overnight?

You have an obligation to set and accomplish your social responsibility objectives, not just out of your obligation to society,
but out of your obligation to the enterprise as well, which depends on society for its existence.

Consider that your business is part of a greater body, and then
ask, "What can we do for the body (the environment [physical or
otherwise], an industry, a community, a city, a region, a nation,
and so on) to help ensure the health of that body?"

7. Profit Requirements

How much profitability do you need?

Your objective cannot be to maximize profit; rather, you must answer this question: What is the minimum needed to achieve all of our objectives? The minimum needed may be much more than your current results or targets. You can only adequately set profit objectives when you know what you will need in order to accomplish your other objectives.

Profit is your business's lifeblood; it is a requirement for survival; it's the cost of staying in business.

Accelerate Innovation and Growth With Stretch Targets for Management and Sales

There are usually two forecast numbers created and discussed for collective teams and individual producers in the management of new sales revenue. One is a "protected" and conservative number, and this is often primarily for the use of the CFO and production. The other is a quota number that is used to manage the team or producers toward acceptable, average, or expected levels of production. This quota number, though, is often the only focus for the producers; it is a number that often defines mediocrity and produces mediocre results.

SMART objectives are:

✓ **S**pecific
✓ **M**easurable
✓ **A**ccountable
✓ **R**ealistically challenging
✓ **T**imed

We must emphasize the importance of "realistically challenging" objectives, so that targets focus on what is possible, not just probable. This is one of the simplest and most effective ways to get a team out of the morass of mediocrity and onto the road of innovation and improvement—which, ultimately, fosters greater growth.

The Danger of Quotas

What do your quotas represent today? Do they represent what is excellent in sales achievement or what is the minimal expectation? And what does a focus on quotas do for sales achievement? In my experience, quotas do one thing excellently: foster mediocrity. In other words, quotas help teams to reach the "cream of the crap."

You have probably heard of sandbagging, but unless you have worked in or around sales, and experienced firsthand mediocre management and quota systems, you have no idea how often it happens and how much it limits the potential for growth in a business. Most of your employees, but especially your sales team, have the desire to know that they are safe in their job. In their quest for security they will quickly trade the potential for the team's optimal growth in exchange for their own personal security. This is why they will do whatever it takes to fight an ever-rising quota, or to ensure that next year, quarter, or month is "off to a good start" with pieces of business that are already "in the bag."

This is another reason why the power of a greater purpose via an inspiring mission with meaning can be a powerful force in riveting a team's focus on the greater good of their team as opposed to their individual desires.

Your job is to consider how you can build the sense of security that your team legitimately has in exchange for getting the most from them. Think about what you can justifiably promise, protect, or deliver to your team that will enhance their sense of security.

Obviously there are times when the fire must be lit underneath them, and jobs may be on the line, but plenty of well-published best practices suggest putting underperformers on a performance plan or getting outplacement for employees ill-suited to their role. Our focus here is on getting sales producers and others to focus on the highest potential production, thus implementing the optimal amount of innovation for greatly accelerated growth.

To do this, you must facilitate the creation of the "Third Number"—a stretch target in almost every area of the company. You do this by asking, "What is the highest potential target we might be able to deliver in regard to this objective? This might assume positive outcomes in the economy, suppliers, future innovations, and so on, but if all the stars were to align, what might we be capable of delivering?"

Identify the Critical Success Factor in Every Strategic Growth Objective

One of most important questions for you to continually ask yourself, for you to ask your team as their manager, and for sales managers to ask sales producers, is the Critical Success Factor (CSF) question: "What is the single most important, **measurable activity** that, if increased in **quantity or quality**, will most accelerate progress toward reaching the growth objective?" A key word in the question is *measurable*, as you must note where performance is now and where it needs to be in the future. In a continuously improving environment you will naturally evolve to a different CSF in time—sometimes within weeks; other times within months or longer. The key to effective and continuous improvement is to constantly move on to the next most important CSF.

After setting an objective, ask the owners of that objective what they believe the CSF to be. Follow up by asking when the optimal level of performance on that CSF might be achieved. Then continue to ask, "What might the next CSF be after this one is accomplished?" And so on. You must have this dialogue both in the planning stage and in your follow-through. These types of CSF-focused conversations are often the heart of any dialogue in consulting, coaching, management, sales management, and even discussions with customers.

Spreadsheets with the measures, accountabilities, and timeline, target deadlines, or other related dates can be used in tracking progress in the improved measures as well as tracking each progressive CSF.

The CSF question can also apply to optimizing almost anyone in his or her role effectiveness, and not just with objectives. Ask yourself: "What is the single most important measurable activity that I most need to improve in quantity or quality, which, when improved, will most accelerate my progress toward being more effective in my role?"

The Socratic approach is usually the optimal way to elicit the most buy-in as well as the higher CSF targets. People tend to not only support that which they help to create, but they also tend to imagine a higher potential in their performance than others may be able to see. In those instances when you believe an individual is capable of accomplishing more than he is saying, first ask him if it is possible that he could achieve the potential CSF level you are envisioning. You may learn of a constraint that he has of which you were unaware, and you may be able to help coach him around that or eliminate it all together. Then you can again work back through the questioning, and, usually without ever telling someone what his goal should be, you can Socratically get him to realize it for himself. This is a common coaching best practice of the majority of turnaround leaders.

Set Clear Growth-Focused Metrics for Each of Your Growth Objectives

Objectives need measures, and the gap between where we are and where we aim to be must be clearly defined in order to optimize progress. Most people hesitate to quantify current or potential performance levels, so it is your role as a growth or turnaround facilitator to quickly get estimates on the current performance measure for every objective you set. During the initial objectives clarification process, most of these measures do not need to be terribly precise; common sense will tell you when you have an appropriate estimate. More exact measures can be plugged into your objectives later. I mention this because too often planning is painfully prolonged by giving too much attention to needless details and unnecessary levels of accuracy.

Once you have established approximate baselines, move on to challenging your team as to what the appropriate targets should be and how they could measure progress on the most appropriate intervals. The key here is that you must ensure that an objective can be adequately measured throughout the course of time. How will you and the team be able to tell if you are at 80 percent or 120 percent of where you should be after six months?

You may need to challenge the metrics to ensure that they are focused on optimal performance levels and growth. You might have to reassure your team that the stretch targets and measures are the most optimistic end of your plan and objectives. People should not live in fear of not reaching stretch targets, but they are where the focus should be. Keep your team's focus on what is possible, not just probable.

Set Stretch Timelines Behind Each of Your Growth Objectives

Set two timelines: one for minimum standards and one for stretch outcomes. You want your team to aim to accomplish as many of an objective's deliverables as possible in as short a timeframe as possible. Even if they are struggling to keep up with the timeline this stretch effort helps to bring out the constraints that are preventing such performance. You can then begin to work on ameliorating the impact of the constraints and, if necessary, adjust the timelines.

To protect your team from burning out, and to keep balance in the effort to accelerate delivery upon the objectives and stretch timelines, don't be afraid to adjust the timelines as time goes on. If delivery upon the stretch timelines is falling short, ask those responsible what they think the new stretch target should be. Sometimes the worst that happens is that the original non-stretch timeline is what was hit, but in the process several constraints were discovered and innovated upon. Improvements were made and ultimately productivity was improved by aggressive goal-setting and accelerated innovation.

Set Optimally Balanced Accountabilities Behind Each of Your Growth Objectives

Knowledge workers aren't in need of babysitting as much as creative stimulation that encourages innovation and improvement. If you set up innovation pairs, teams, or committees and tie accountabilities to meeting agendas, you'll find it helps to not only keep progress on course but also get people to raise the bar and think and create differently than they would alone.

We accomplish accountability in our innovation workshops and strategic growth facilitations through quarterly public review of progress and the individual stretch plans each manager has created. Every participant prioritizes the top three or so areas of innovation and/or objectives they feel they could make a personal impact upon. Their managers receive a copy of these innovation stretch plans, and progress is also often reported in regular management meetings.

Growth Objectives From the Bottom Up

On many occasions, I have had the opportunity to work with a strong visionary leader who had specific, aggressive objectives that even he or she thought to be a stretch. But after conducting some basic research with that company and its customers it became apparent to me that I needed to recommend a strategy that would be a bit of a shock to the visionary leader. My advice, to that leader and to you, is to *not* give your idea of what the targets should be, but instead to first listen to what the individual team members, and especially individual sales producers, think their target growth objectives should be. The team's target is usually even higher than the leader's.

You will experience several benefits from listening to the individual units and/or sales team producers present their growth objectives before you present your targets. First, if the collective total is greater than your target, you will avoid missing out on what your dictated targets would have accomplished—a lower result. Odds are a team will hit the target given them. This is a great example of why hitting a goal can be the height of failure. Second, you will learn insights in the process. Your team will share new insights with you as to why things may or may not be realistic. Throughout the process you can address and rectify misperceptions.

You can know where you'll need to adjust resources, because you listened first. Thirdly, people tend to support that which they help to create. So your team is more likely to follow through on plans and targets they were a part of creating, as opposed to those you are simply dictating.

Time and time again, presidents and managers are shocked at how much higher the individuals on a team will collectively set their own team or individual objectives than if an objective is dictated to them. This strategy will not only raise the bar of your sales targets, but revenues, productivity, and profits as well.

Accelerate Growth by Turning Managers Into Strategic Growth Coaches

Your challenge is to get your managers focused on what matters most. You must have a practice for getting these managers out of the tyranny of the urgent, myopic minutiae and into high-impact areas of focus that are too often pushed to the back burner by a lack of urgency.

Every manager by the very definition of his or her title is responsible for getting workers to become more effective. Whether your managers are excellent sources of best-practice wisdom for those reporting to them or not, you can still get your managers to become more effective at managing by beginning the practice of Growth Coaching Sessions. The purpose of these sessions is to have the manager discuss areas such as:

✓ The growth objectives to which their direct reports are responsible.

✓ What the CSF is for each objective, and what measurable activities most need to be improved.

✓ Innovation areas and progress in them.

✓ Role-related questions from the roles tools in Chapter 2.

The bottom line is, getting managers to coach employees on the strategic growth objectives will improve their management effectiveness and productivity.

Prioritizing or Defining One Central Growth Objective

I surveyed hundreds of top managers and owners of companies about having a clear central growth objective, or CGO, and these were some of the results.

✓ 66% of the companies we surveyed don't have a CGO, but think that they should.

✓ Of the companies that had a CGO, only 32% regularly communicated their progress.

✓ Of the companies that had a CGO, only 28% had a realistically challenging one.

✓ Only 14% of companies are creatively engaging their customer to accelerate their progress toward the CGO.

✓ 100% were certain they could exceed their current performance!

If all the stars were to align and your team were to implement some significant improvements and innovations, what is the incremental growth you envision your team could experience, and what would be the best measure of that growth? Market share, gross revenues or profits, net profitability, participation in deals for your market, or some other specific objective for your organization?

It's amazing the growth we have seen at companies that for three generations were more than happy with 10 percent and sometimes even just 5 percent annual growth. Other companies have smugly said, "We are growing at 30/40/50 percent per year, we don't need to improve anything." And yet when companies of both of these types of growth patterns have stepped back and gone through an accelerated growth workshop and facilitation process for the purpose optimizing revenues and profits, their teams innovated significant incremental improvements to the current growth pattern.

In that same survey, we found that despite agreement from the respondents that the following were key best practices in accelerating growth, the vast majority of organizations failed to successfully implement any of them. How does your company stack up?

Sample Central Growth Objective Survey

- ✓ Do you have a specific Central Growth Objective that is understood by everyone on your team?
- ✓ Is your CGO realistically challenging and believable?
- ✓ Is the CGO exciting, inspiring, emotionally charged, and full of purpose? Does it call your team to action, or is it just another directive?
- ✓ Are your metrics charted, graphed, and visually fed back in shorter (monthly or more frequently) as opposed to longer periods of time, to all of your team?
- ✓ Is an objective third party challenging you and the team to raise the bar, dispelling any skepticism of aggressive growth, and ensuring open communication?
- ✓ Is your CGO built not top-down, but by consensus, with a representative set of objective inputs from throughout your team?
- ✓ Is a representation of your customer base invited to give insights on improvement, and are customers' challenges invited through one-on-one open dialogue, ideally

with a third party (as opposed to strictly quantitative surveying tactics)?

In over 20 years of working with management, sales, marketing, and customers to facilitate turnarounds and faster rates of growth, I've seen the identification and clarification of a CGO often be the key leverage point. Even the best of companies with excellent track records consistently make significant improvements when they challenge themselves to raise the bar. It's not magic, but rather a simple process of strategy that isn't often fully implemented. Two things help to ensure the effectiveness of the effort. First: either having a strong internal sponsor or a third party who is thoroughly experienced with the process and is involved in facilitating, coaching, challenging, and holding accountable those who are the stewards of the growth objectives. Second: involving the customer to keep the process customer-centric and focused on increasing the value for the customer.

If your strategic plan doesn't come as close to this chapter's seven key points as you want it to, you probably don't have a fully fleshed and aggressive growth plan. If you are a steward of growth and are unsure whether an adequate Central Growth Objective and process have been implemented, pass out the CGO survey, or contact me for a link to an online version. Challenge your leadership to raise the bar and make this the fastest-growing time in your company's history, just as so many other companies are experiencing right now.

Chapter 4
Growth Strategy and Turnaround as a Continuous Process

Strategy is a process, not an event.

The reason many companies are in need of turnaround is that their strategy is neither process-oriented nor adequately communicated. I've seen well-made, valid plans that have failed chiefly because no one outside of the top leadership team could adequately communicate what the strategy was—especially the areas in which they had a part to play. How many in your team could answer the question, "What are the top strategic objectives to which you have a contribution, and how well are you doing right now at meeting each of those objectives for this quarter and the year?"

Just the process of thoroughly communicating and dialoging about your objectives can be transformational for your team.

When your business strategy is clear and concise, it can bring focus to every facet of an organization. When your objectives are not well communicated throughout the organization, or, worse yet, are nebulous, this will beget dysfunction and incongruity. I have seen turnaround experts who had no experience in an industry succeed chiefly because of their thoroughness of communication throughout the company. When it comes to your strategy and objectives, it is far better to over-communicate the targets and progress.

If your team has looked at the strategy process as a once-a-year leadership retreat where you set top objectives and do some teambuilding, then you haven't been looking at more than one step of a much longer ongoing journey. If the setting of those objectives is mostly left to input from top management and hasn't involved customer input and most or all of your team, then you've left potential for greater buy-in to chance and reduced your odds of success. Involving more people in the process of creation of objectives will increase buy-in. Here are several approaches you can use to involve more of your team members and make it more of a process.

Focus on Quarter-by-Quarter Progress and Realignment

Have you ever set key growth objectives only to see them fade into the background of your team's focus? Has the tyranny of the urgent too often distracted the attention needed to make regular progress on your objectives? Just as publicly held companies have a focus on quarterly progress, your company should have a quarterly reporting of progress to your employees and perhaps other key stakeholders. Wall Street demands quarterly updates for the purposes of investment, and having a quarterly focus on milestones and progress has tremendous managerial and even psychological benefits as well. Strategies are always imperfect. Corrections and adjustments will inevitably need to be made to your objectives, and quarterly progress reports allow for these corrections to be made before it's too late. I've been shocked at the number of times I've heard companies share that they didn't change the strategy or a key objective after it had become irrelevant because the review of the strategy wasn't due until the end of the year.

Psychologically, a quarterly reporting of progress, and re-alignment as needed, keeps your team focused and reminded of objectives that might otherwise be forgotten until it is too late. Frankly, many objectives are best reported monthly or even in real time, but quarterly should be a minimum reporting and realignment touch point. Creating milestones that chart the appropriate progress every three months also gives people enough time to focus on the non-urgent but highly important work that must be tended to on a quarter-by-quarter basis. People can typically envision three months out with ease: "It's just the month after the month after next...hey, I better get working on this now before it gets too late!"

In regard to sales or other production-oriented objectives, I recommend that you make the reporting of progress as close to real-time as possible. For example, in sales, it is quite easy to create a bar chart of progress for the organization, teams, and individuals. Showing these bar charts of progress on a week-to-week basis can help to motivate people to get caught up or even aim to be ahead of the pack. You should be careful of using just a spreadsheet to report such data though; many individuals don't process numbers well and have a tough time putting the relevant numbers in perspective. You will want to use bar or other types of charts that show a percent of progress toward the goal as it relates to the quarter, the year, and to the rest of the team. When people see that they are behind the pack or that they are behind where they should be for being 25, 50, or 75 percent of the way through the year, they can still have time to catch up.

Keeping Perspective With the Seasons

If your business has high and low cycles throughout the year, you will want to be sure that you put that perspective into your progress targets and charts. I am amazed at companies who just break down the expected production to an equal 25 percent per quarter, "because that is the way we would like production to be: evenly spread among each quarter so that the rest of us aren't burdened by sales' inability to sell equally in every quarter." The fact is that many businesses have seasonal undulations that are best accounted for into each quarter's milestone objectives. Sales teams will tend to sandbag and save deals for a future quarter or month when they are sure to hit the target and garner their full commission. Often the fourth quarter is the busiest, and whether this makes sense to you or not, it is a fact that is best weighed into that quarter's target numbers. Your goal is to get the optimal realistic levels of productivity from every time period.

Once the annual target has been bought into it is best to get individual commitments on quarter-by-quarter targets. Where it is practical, get each individual to agree and set what his or her individual quarter-by-quarter milestones should be, as there may be variances from territory to territory. This will engender optimal buy-in, commitment, and follow-through.

Use Customer Depth Interviews

It is essential to involve customers in the process of setting objectives. You won't be asking them to set your objectives directly, but their input can illuminate the potential opportunities around which your objectives can be set. I will give more detail on the customer depth interview process in Chapter 6, but for now, when making your turnaround and growth strategy more of a continuous improvement process, you must include regular customer input each quarter. Customer input from open-ended qualitative discussions is not a once-a-year project but an ongoing effort that is a requirement of every strategic process.

Depending on your size and ability, determine an appropriate number of customers that you will interview each quarter. You may also include key suppliers in your interviews each quarter. You will want these interviews to explore areas that relate to your strategy and any progress you are or are not making each quarter.

Without open-ended customer input every quarter, you do not have a strategy process. Ensuring that this customer input is gathered and shared quarterly can help to keep you nimble and responsive so that you won't miss out on opportunities.

The same customers won't necessarily be interviewed every quarter, but some may. Ideally you want to be getting a wide variety of insights on your strategic progress and competitive positioning, so a quarter-by-quarter variety of customer input will be beneficial. You will soon see how customers will be impressed by your following up on a regular basis on the areas covered in past interviews.

Involve All of Your Team

Many online tools are available to measure how your team views your company's performance in key areas and ranks the priorities for growth. Which tools you use is not as important as using *something* that gathers all of your team's insights into performance and the priority of areas and objectives in need of attention and improvement. You could create a simple printed question-naire or an online survey from many of the online tools available. My company has successfully used both the customized online tools and the most simple of printed surveys to gather this input. The key is that you listen to your team and consistently give them the opportunity to give their feedback on what needs attention.

Surveys are a double-edged sword. When teams take a survey there is a skepticism that often ensues, because often little to no response is ever given back to the team. You must be certain to give some type of feedback on what was learned and what types of actions are likely to be taken. The best course of action is to not only survey and give feedback, but then also show progress on the new objectives that were set and are being worked on because of the team's input. When team members see that they are not only listened to but that their input is making a difference, they are greatly enthused to give more and more constructive feedback and look for opportunities where they can impact change and improvement.

Many companies experience good results by having at least a quarterly conversation with all or most of the team to discuss progress, constraints, and next steps in the strategy. Other teams benefit more from a monthly session. Determine what is best for your situation and ensure that the team will respond back to you that "communication about our progress on the strategy is good."

Going Off-Site to Get in Sync and on Course

Have you noticed how often leadership teams are distracted with the minutiae of their work? Has it been difficult to get managers to be fully focused during planning meetings because work was screaming out for their attention? A simple tool you can use to capture the focus of the leadership team is to take them off-site every 6 weeks for a half-day, full day, or even two days of meeting to discuss and plan the growth and turnaround strategy. This may sound like a tremendous amount of time, and it is, but is there anything else more important than having your top leadership totally focused on turning around your company and optimizing growth? It can be as simple and inexpensive as reserving a room at your local library, art museum, or a state park, and it can be for as little as five hours. The symbolism and practicality of a meeting with such focus can be quite impactful.

In the initial stages I may have leadership teams go off-site once a month. Later, every six weeks seems to be enough frequency for the leadership team to discuss more intently and intimately the key issues that might not otherwise be addressed in weekly management meetings, such as the health of the culture, the progress on key objectives, the level of sustained innovation, and the key marketing decisions that affect market standing, market focus, and customer intimacy.

Prioritizing Objectives

As a leader or facilitator of a team you may not yet have the insight and clarity to know what improvement opportunities should have the most urgent focus and priority. It might not be clear to you (or any of the top leaders) what objectives or issues demand the highest attention. So, it is a good practice to use a tool for ranking areas of opportunity. Even if you are certain of the correct ranking, involving the team in the process will increase the likelihood of success. Forgive my repetition on this point, but it is critical: People tend to support that which they help to create.

For many years my company has used some form of online survey to assess what the CEO, management team, and employees as separate groups are viewing to be the priorities for improvement. We assess both the performance and priority ranking of a few dozen areas and compare the results from the three entities. CEOs are usually far too optimistic about the performance levels in the various areas, management is usually less optimistic, and the employees give the harshest—and often the most accurate—assessments on performance. There are various and sundry online assessments to choose from, though nothing replaces 360-degree depth interviews throughout a good portion of the organization and customer base. There is one online toolset in particular that I have found to be holistic enough to use, and is a good addendum to interviews. It allows our consultants to have a view and metrics as if we were a "virtual CEO." If you contact my office we will be glad to provide access to that toolset. Having been certified with those assessments and intimately familiar with them, we can provide a discount as well as guidance in their use. Without such guidance, I suspect that tools such as these can become a crutch, a distraction, and an addiction in the process of strategy outlined in this book.

I also interview a sampling of representatives throughout the company to look for themes in opportunities and constraints. Often management is blind to the root cause of key problems, so having a third party open a candid and confidential conversation with the rank and file can quickly elicit the root issues. Thus I recommend that you have both quantitative and qualitative feedback mechanisms as part of any turnaround or accelerated growth effort. Quantitative feedback will show that communication is a problem, and qualitative feedback will turn up things like, for example, the fact that "the plant manager, even though he doesn't mean to be, is coming off very harsh and rude to people who bring up any problems, and he is the central constraint to our communication issues."

We use high-end proprietary software and hardware tools in the consulting world to quickly get teams to rank the priority and impact levels of issues and objectives. If you don't have the time or resources to use these tools you can do something as simple as having breakout group lunch meetings where you can ask for simple priority weightings, such as "1 to 10" or "A, B, or C." The key is to ask and be open to their feedback in order to optimize their support of the turnaround effort. Safety in communicating with candor is always a priority in a turnaround.

The Growth Power of Knowing Your Constraints

How open are you to discussing your company's greatest problems? Do you consistently ask for your employees' feedback on what the biggest problems are in the company, or do you avoid these discussions because you feel that you get the same answers and you disagree with the areas of concern? Do you have an open-door policy and mature, adult attitudes throughout the management team that ensure that you are fully aware of the top constraints, problems, and opportunities affecting your growth? Having a quarterly "opportunities discussion" for employees to share these types of issues can help to nip problems in the bud as well as fuel an effective innovation process.

Besides setting objectives and coaching your team through progressively advancing critical success factors (CSFs, detailed in Chapter 3), you must also always be looking for the *opposite* of the positive targets. The opposite of progress towards a target, or anything that is unnecessarily slowing your progress, is a constraint. Business is nothing but a series of processes and relationships lined up next to each other, and in every process there is a flow-through point that is smaller than the others. Just as with a pipe delivering a liquid, where the flow is only as great as the most constrained point of the piping, every business process has a most pressing constraint. These constraints will usually become connected to an objective's CSF: The CSF is the measurable activity that, if improved, would most accelerate progress toward the objective;

the constraint is the issue that is most slowing delivery of a desired result. As you identify your most constricting factors and solve them or lessen their impact more and more quickly, you will accelerate growth.

To get to the bottom of your constraints you must become the master of looking for, asking about, and prioritizing constraints for intervention. You must foster a culture that is open to discussing the problems, challenges, and constraints with as much openness as you have in discussing objectives. Just as I noted in the first chapter, finding and innovating around your constraints as fast as possible is a key to turnaround success and the optimization of growth and profits. At some clients we have mapped out all of the critical processes of the business and regularly ask, "What is currently the most pressing constraint on this process, and what should we be doing about eliminating or lessening the impact of that constraint?"

Consider hanging up these maps and inviting your team to post sticky notes with ideas or challenges to generate more ideas around the constraints. Keep the focus on continuous improvement by making visually available what is in need of attention and you will get more and more input.

Be sure to put more focus on innovating out the weaknesses of the *process*—not any weaknesses of your people. And by reinforcing and praising the strengths of your *people*—not the strengths of the process—your people and your processes will *both* improve.

Continuously looking for the most constrained part of the process is one focus needed to increase output.

Chapter 5
Echeloned Service Impressions

Often in a challenging business situation with poor sales revenues and poor customer retention, internal service breakdowns are negatively influencing customers' perceptions of service quality. The following steps will guide your team through transforming not only the customers' experience, but also the attitude employees will have about service priorities, values, and processes, ultimately leading to improved customer retention and profits.

Successfully putting in place a process that will ensure an excellent service impression with customers can in and of itself be the tipping point in a turnaround. An excellent service impression with customers is something that can be created or destroyed merely by the quality and frequency of your team's communication with customers. Being that communication alone has such a powerful impact on this impression, this area can be one of the most cost-effective strategies for facilitating a turnaround via improving customer retention.

In most turnaround situations the service impression and positioning with many customers is going to be negative. Yet despite how bad your current service impressions may be, there is hope for repositioning your service as excellent in the minds of your customers. You will need to identify where you are currently, what the key influencers are with your customers, and what innovations, if implemented, will have the greatest impression (while staying within the constraints of your limited resources).

Assess Your Customers' Impressions

Survey a selection of customers—past, current, and future—on the following areas:

- ✓ How satisfied are they with your service?
- ✓ How does your service impression compare with the competition's service impression?
- ✓ Where are your service strengths and improvement opportunities?
- ✓ What will it take to improve the service impressions you are making, and what is the value of that improved service to the customer?

If you have enough territories with varying levels of service quality, you will want to find out not just the reasons for the differences but what the value to your company is for improved service performance. You may be able to determine that increasing customer service impression levels from an average of a 6 to an 8 on a 10 scale improves customer retention by 50 percent. Improved customer retention may be worth many times the minor investments you may need to make to innovate and improve your service levels in the lagging territories. Determine—and communicate to your team—the value of increased customer retention through improved service impressions. When your team understands the impact of service impressions they will be more likely to optimize them.

For prospective customers you can use a service impression survey as a marketing and prospecting tool. You want to uncover what it will take to get and keep customers, and in surveying prospective customers you can often find qualified leads for your sales team. You will learn what it is they need to hear to be sold and you will learn what service levels are expected to keep their business.

Know the Potentials—Industry Bests and Averages

Benchmark your industry and find out how highly rated your best competitors are in service impressions. Determine if exceeding their service level impressions is the right objective. The majority of the time I find our clients can easily beat out their industry's service exemplars with the use of the service strategies we discuss here. The point though is that your team must know that these targets are realistic, and that slight, incremental improvements in service level impressions are not the objective. Rather, you want your team to think of nothing less than a full service-level impression turnaround. Usually you can also prove this is a realistic objective to your service teams by finding the people on your team who are already topping the competition's exemplars.

Set Your Service Objectives

Once you've uncovered the industry best practices and the ratings of top-echelon service-level impressions, share the results with your team. Involve those on your team who can affect the service scores in setting specific objectives and aggressive timelines toward which they are willing to aim.

Often areas like customer retention are directly impacted by service-level impressions. Set objectives in these areas as part of your service turnaround strategy. Customer retention is a great example of an area so valuable that it would probably make economic sense to tie incentives to this area of objectives and give bonuses to those who are impacting service-level impressions and customer retention. Even minor rewards and recognition on service improvements and the resulting impact can go a long way to sustaining the improved behaviors.

Stealing From Your
Competition—Legally

I've met more than a few turnaround specialists whose favorite tactic for improving sales and service teams was to ask customers and prospects the following questions:

- ✓ Who is your favorite service tech?
- ✓ What do you like most about the service from the competition?
- ✓ If we could deliver on the promise of topping their service levels would you switch to our solutions?

The next step is to hire the best service techs and sales reps from the competition, by paying them what they are worth. This, along with genuine improvements in the service levels, makes the necessary impression to win back old customers and win over new customers.

No matter how bad of a situation you are in regarding past service-level impressions, if you can have confidence that significant improvements can be made, odds are you can win back lost customers. I know of one situation in which the new owner of a company quickly discovered that every major customer of his had already decided to bolt for the competition. Quotes like "I'll never let our company do business with yours for as long as I live" were common. The total value of his company was lost as this represented more than 90 percent of revenues. He had only one tool and one promise, and that was his "One Chance Close." He went out to every lost customer and told them just how bad his situation was, and how poor the service and quality had been at the company throughout the past year. He actually gave them more bad news and reports about his newly purchased company's past service failures. He expressed understanding, saying that he would leave too if he was in his customer's situation, and then described how he planned to turn things around. He asked this question: "I know you have had a terrible experience, and you have every reason to leave, but because I am a new owner, and because I have a specific plan to address every service failure you experienced, will you give me just one chance to make things right?" He reengaged every lost customer and built that company from less than $1 million to more than $100 million in short order.

When Service Quality Is Not Job 1

A commonly accepted syllogism in business is this: Of the three pillars of competitive advantage—quality, service, and price—you can only be competitive in two categories, and you must consciously make this strategic decision or risk losing focus and growth potential. There will be times when quality and price may be the points of advantage on which you have decided to compete. In this case though you will certainly not promote that your service is bad, but instead that your quality and price more than make up for it. This is a perfect example of where you can beat the competition by doing a better job at creating better service *impressions* without necessarily having superior service.

It's *impression*, not reality.

I purposely use the phrase *service-level impression* to make the point that what the customer experiences with your team is nothing more than an impression, and does not necessarily represent a markedly different level of actual service or investment on your part. The point here is that service-level impressions are made in how your employees communicate, listen, and respond to customers—more so than measurable things like parts availability, response times, or order accuracy. Every company makes mistakes, but it is how you respond to them that often sets you on top with higher service-level impressions. The simplest of changes and low-cost investments can put your company in the very best light and leave the impression that no competitor's service levels come close to yours.

What makes the best impressions on your customers? In most industries there are a few commonalities amongst customers as to what makes them feel well served. High in the priority list are things such as:

✓ **Prompt response to the first phone call** about problems and requests, with little to no hold times, and always being able to reach a live support person, even if it is only the person at the front desk, directing the call

✓ **Thoroughness in communication**, telling a customer specifically what he or she can expect, and, of course, under-promising and over-delivering when you can be confident of the response.

✓ **Frequency of communication.** In some industries we have seen how a daily update call on, for example, the stage of repair of an item, or an explanation of the next effort to fix the problem is all that is needed to out-impress the competition that may actually have speedier service or better quality.

✓ **Service promises and commitments.** Making service-level promises or guarantees on response times, parts availability, or what your company will do if a service promise can't be kept can help to overcome a genuine gap between your service and the competitors'.

✓ **Accessibility to the top.** Customers are impressed by having the ability to reach the president of the company, or the plant manager, or some other high-ranking official, if a service problem reaches a disconcerting level. With some of our clients we have actually printed the president's or owner's cell phone numbers onto service commitment marketing collateral—it is powerfully persuasive for a sales rep to say, "What other competitor is going to have enough confidence in their service to give the president's cell phone number to every customer?"

Impression of Service Quality

By increasing the frequency of contact with dissatisfied customers and allowing them to reach higher levels of authority you can actually increase their impression of service quality.

You have probably heard of the practice at high-quality hotels of empowering all of their employees to spend up to $1,000 to help a customer or make a great impression. Establishing such dollar limits is something that most companies need to do, but the escalation strategy can go a step further.

A best practice in service excellence is to implore employees to deny (almost) no customer requests, to never tell a customer "no." Whereas it might be feasible to never reject a customer return when you are selling shoes or clothing, the return of a $250,000 software implementation or piece of machinery is another matter. This strategy involves leveraging your company's chain of command.

When a front-line service person can't satisfy a customer's request, the practice is to allow the customer to make his or her appeal to a higher authority. Determine the best chain of command to escalate such calls, as well as the appropriate maximum level of calls a customer might go through. The higher an issue is taken, usually the more adroit the manager is and the more able they are at addressing the concern and ameliorating the customer's frustration. The higher a customer concern goes, the more attention the root issue gets, preventing the issue from occurring again.

The other benefit of the escalation strategy is that the customer at least feels listened to and heard. As many service improvement programs will teach, it is about ensuring that the customer feels totally listened to, that he or she has been given the ability to vent. Another result of this strategy that I see is a significant percentage of customers who not only dial back the intensity of their emotion, but also the assertiveness of their request and their overall dissatisfaction with the company.

Marketing Your Distinctive Service

Once you have begun to execute on some of these service strategies, focus on pumping up the positioning of your service through your marketing and sales communications. Many companies offer service no different from any of their competition, but because they heavily promote their "unique" service values, commitments, promises, and stories, the market begins to believe that they have the best service. A few well-told stories in marketing material or through your sales force can begin the process of branding your commitment to better service. You may want to consider confessing past service failures and explaining what you are doing to facilitate a turnaround. This can be a very successful angle if executed correctly.

Incentivizing Service Excellence

Consider creative or significant incentives for your team that are well promulgated. The more attention you give service, and the more you inspect what you expect, the more service will get respect.

Maintaining Service Excellence

Certain of your essential areas of objectives may also require you to set service-related objectives, such as in the innovation and productivity objectives. The specifics may pertain to the appropriate service levels and improvement required to reach your growth objectives or the amount of innovation and repositioning that service needs to receive to reach the appropriate service-level impressions.

Fix Internal Service Breakdowns to Stop External Breakdowns

Often the cause of poor service impressions with customers is the breakdown of the culture or processes inside a company. Employees can be quick to let the frustrations of internal company problems show through in their own impatience with customers. You must be sure to educate your team as to how they serve each other and who their internal customers are—and that you are holding them accountable to the same service values inside as they are expected to deliver on the outside.

Incorporating service-oriented commitments into the corporate values is also essential to reaffirming the service commitment and maintaining a healthy, ongoing focus on quality service impression. Once you know you are improving, innovating, and better positioning your service-level impressions, then accelerated growth and turnaround will soon follow.

Internal customer service is often the first requirement of external customer service excellence.

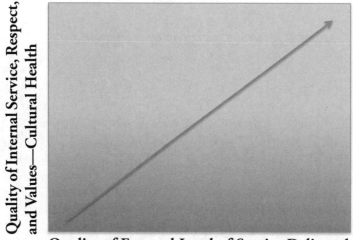

Quality of External Level of Service Delivered to Customers, and Employee Attitude

Improving the internal service culture improves external service.

Chapter 6
Echeloned Depth Interviews

Strategically Mining Customer Potential

How much untapped potential lies within your existing customer base? For most companies the current customer base is a significant percentage of existing revenue and can also be a key step to accelerated growth or a turnaround. Using a third party to conduct depth interviews with customers is de rigueur for the strategic planning process, and if you aren't having depth interviews conducted with customers, your company is missing out on one of the most valuable aspects of a full strategic planning process. Depth interviews can play a key role in fostering innovation, garnering untapped sales, and helping to differentiate your company in the marketplace.

Finding the potential within your top customer relationships is one of the most valuable and high-ROI efforts your business can invest in. But too often divining that potential is left to the selling efforts of business development, sales, and service teams that lack the ability to uncover the full value of customer relationships. You may have qualified individuals on your team who could conduct depth interviews with customers, but the very fact that they are part of the organization that they are analyzing can taint the objectivity of the process and the fullness of input from the customers.

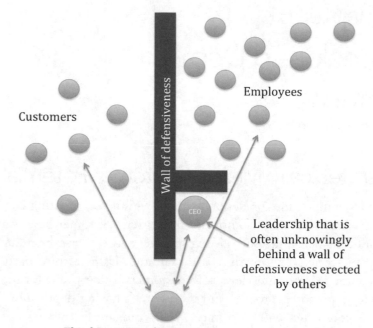

Third Party Depth Interviewers can get
access to insights others cannot

What Depth Interviews
Are and Are Not

Depth interviews are basically guided one-on-one conversations conducted by a third party to gather insights about what the
customer values, and what the customer perceives about you and
your competition. Ideally they should be conducted face to face
with open time limits, but they can effectively be conducted on
the phone when time is of essence.

After introducing myself, I segue into depth interviews I'm
conducting with my client's customers usually by saying, "I'm

conducting an innovation and service improvement initiative for my client and they have retained our company to gather insights from their best customers as to what is most important to the customers, how they view my client's performance, and where my client could innovate the next improvements that might dynamically improve customers' situations." Nearly all of those we contact are delighted to invest the time and greatly appreciate the fact that their opinion is being valued so highly. The process cements good customer relationships.

Depth interviews are not used to conduct any direct selling, although new sales potentials usually are a result. They are not quantitative surveys gathering tedious rankings, scales, or grades from the customer on your past performance. Although you may occasionally ask for some measures, the questions you will have created for a depth interview will not require gathering much hard, quantifiable data.

The Limitations of Traditional Interviewing Techniques

Sales and Service Teams

It is true that your sales and service teams are motivated to sell additional products and services, but they are rarely incentivized to innovate the products, services, or methodologies of the business. They aren't motivated or empowered to look for what could lead to much greater growth than the stepped sales improvements on which they focus. They often lack the savvy to discuss areas of a strategic nature or the macro picture of the customer and industry, and they may lack the political abilities or awareness about their organization to know just what your company's potentials for innovation and improvement are.

Customers are often reluctant to give sales reps information that can be used as ammunition against them in pricing negotiations. Customers are frequently more tight-lipped with salespeople than anyone else, even if the relationship is relatively healthy. The insiders on your team will also lack objectivity compared to what an outsider can bring to the discussion with your customers.

Focus Groups

Because of these handcuffs that are on most sales and service staff, oftentimes focus groups and classic qualitative research are used to assess service levels and other areas of concern. But focus groups force customers to only share the information they have no fear of sharing publicly. However, the most valuable information for innovation and discovering incremental sales within a customer relationship is usually of a confidential nature. The challenges that lie within these relationships are not the things that most people would feel comfortable discussing publicly. Marketing researchers lament how often focus groups result in a groupthink and are often dominated by the strong personalities within each group.

Surveys

Voice-of-customer, qualitative interviews, and other similar surveys can do an excellent job of assessing service levels and customer concerns; the problem lies in the savvy that the interviewers may or may not have, as well as the objectives of the qualitative research. Interviewers rarely have the combination of sales, strategy, and innovation savvy that can enable them to parlay information into more significant incremental revenue and profitability improvements.

The objectives of qualitative research are typically not focused on uncovering the incremental sales and innovation potential in the relationships and overall market. Usually, qualitative research is used to assess past performance levels and test new product ideas that are already developed.

The Ideal Interviewer

What is needed to uncover the fullest potential of the customer relationship is a set of skills, experience, and foci that allows for the maximization of your partnership with the customer—skills for asking questions that assess the overall strategy, specific areas of objectives, and the vision of the potential of your customer relationships and other innovations. The interviewer ideally should have experience and savvy in speaking with the C-level executives of all sizes of customer companies as well as your own team.

The interviewer must have the ability to express the objective of taking the existing relationship from its current level to a much larger partnership for mutual objectives. They need to be able to focus on the customers' and stakeholders' ideal outcomes that might lead to growth in value, revenues, and profits from your relationship—not just for your company but for all the stakeholders in the partnership. The goal is to expand the pie for all, not just get a bigger piece.

Qualitative interviews focus on the results of the past, and not the potentials of the future. Too often even the more experienced consultants and marketing staff focus on assessing past successes and shortcomings. Sometimes, because of a lack of experience in selling, management, strategy, and innovation, qualitative researchers are not as savvy at asking the essential questions that uncover the potentials of the relationship. *Depth interviews should aim to elicit information from a customer quantifying the value of potential results.*

Another theme that must be included in facilitating quality depth interviews is that of fostering innovation-oriented conversation. It is rare for customers to think too far beyond the paradigm and perceived restrictions of the relationship; therefore, a discussion that is focused on potentials and blue-sky innovative thinking needs to be facilitated through depth interviews. Taking a customer down a path three years into the future, on a road where the customer can clearly envision the untapped potentials that exceed current expectations—this is the type of discussion seldom facilitated, yet most needed. Too often we are more concerned with surveys that measure performance, or selling and servicing to meet this quarter's quota.

In discerning whom to engage to facilitate true depth interviews, and how to unlock the fuller potential of customer relationships, there are several factors to consider:

- ✓ Does he have experience in consultative questioning, selling, and the ability to dollarize potential value?

- ✓ Will she be able to take the findings of untapped sales potential back to a sales and service team of varying abilities, and coach them in the implementation and realization of these newfound potentials?

- ✓ Is he savvy not just in discussing strategy but also in assisting executives in clarifying previously unthought-of objectives and potentials?

- ✓ Does she have the acumen to draw out these discoveries from the customer, as well as then facilitate the formulation of any strategies needed by the leadership team of your company?

- ✓ Is he knowledgeable at developing innovation programs and processes?

- ✓ Does she have the ability to take amorphous ideas and couch them with specific measurable activities that are calendarized with clear points of accountability and follow-up?

✓ Is he not only a good written communicator, but also effective at vocally relaying the findings to large groups, who will not only need to be apprised of findings, but of the strategies necessary to follow through upon them?

To justify the investment and optimize the process of depth interviews, you should begin by looking at the untapped potential of your top existing customers, especially newer customers who may hold greater growth potential. You don't need an exhaustive list to get started, but a list that is representative. What many of our clients discover is that the retention or expansion of just one good customer more than pays for the investment of retaining our services and the time invested in the depth interview process.

Whom to Interview

We suggest interviewing three customer groups:

1. Champion customers.
2. Highest growth potential customers.
3. Lost customers.

The champions will give us excellent testimonials and insights into the competitive advantages of our client. These insights and testimonials will help in marketing and sales efforts as well as with positioning—how our clients can differentiate themselves in the marketplace. The high growth–potential customers will usually give insights as to what it will take to win more of their business. From these high growth–potential customers we can glean marketing and selling themes that can be leveraged throughout the customer base. This is where the effort more than pays for itself. In fact, we have seen the depth interview process help to bring about nine-figure returns for companies below a half-billion dollars in total revenue. Finally, interviewing a sampling of lost customers helps to uncover opportunities for prevention as well as potentials for recovery.

Once you've compiled a target list for interviews, amalgamate the estimated potential and set objectives for the process. This will help to ensure follow-through on potential innovations and sales. You will want to strategically identify the specific contacts within each customer company who have the most gravitas and influence on your relationship. Ideally they are within the decision-maker team or are the approvers of that team's recommendations. You want to choose interviewees who stand to gain the most from your innovations and the deepening of the partnership. They will be most engaged and open to the process.

What to Ask

You want to create a map of discussion areas regarding your customers' views on:

✓ What they like or dislike about your sales process or service.

✓ What they like and don't like about your competition.

✓ How you compare to the competition.

✓ Their dollar quantification of value for the services you provide them.

✓ What would cause them to leave.

✓ Their additional needs, relative to (and sometimes just beyond the scope of) your relationship.

✓ Their problems or top constraints to growth.

✓ Their ballpark on the "dollarized" value lost or gained based upon the potential innovations in service, products, and relationship.

✓ The economic result of accelerating progress toward their mission-critical objectives. (How does improving their performance, in what they've identified as their own critical success factors for their mission-critical objectives, increase their revenues?)

- ✓ Where they are having problems, not just with your company, but in general.
- ✓ How you could better work together to improve their performance.
- ✓ Their top considerations in buying additional services or products.

Use Depth Interviews to Improve Your Positioning and Competitive Awareness

Most people in marketing, sales, and company leadership are grossly unaware of how their customers view them and the competition. Fostering awareness of your positioning points of uniqueness, advantage, equality, and weakness improves your ability to effectively position your company and increase customer retention. What follows is a way to set up a process of continually improving competitive awareness and understanding your business's positioning points, both of which marketing and sales departments need in order to effectively position your company.

Differentiating Yourself in the Marketplace— Positioning for Accelerated Growth

A frequently asked question from business leadership is, "How do we define and communicate our difference and the aspects about our mission that are unique?" And from that question, "Is there anything that really is unique about one business as opposed to another?" The tool we use to help our clients understand how they differ in the marketplace as well as how to better sell and market their competitive advantage is something we call the Positioning Points Grid. The grid will require input from your team and customers. Building it and maintaining it turns it into a process that helps to foster competitive awareness.

Every company has a mix of positioning points that define how it is better, similar to, or worse than the alternative choices for a customer. We call these **positioning points of uniqueness, advantage, equality,** and **weakness**.

Part of your initial work is to compile a list of your competition and competitive alternatives. You may know of most of your competitors, but the truest lens through which to see your competitors is that of your customer. Regularly asking customers who *and* what are the alternatives to your solutions is something most sales reps fear doing, yet the exercise is powerful and will increase selling effectiveness. Make this a regular part of your depth interview process.

Often companies have "competitors" that are different options, other than actual competitor companies, one "competitor" is the customer making no changes at all. The more competitively aware your team members are, the more effective they become at targeting, questioning, qualifying, positioning, and ultimately closing more business with better profit margins.

Next you will want to begin filling out the grid by asking your team these questions:

- ✓ What do we offer the customer that no one else offers? (Your **points of competitive uniqueness**)
- ✓ What do we offer that is demonstratively better than the competition? (**Points of competitive advantage**)
- ✓ Where are we equal with our competitors? (**Points of equality**)
- ✓ What are our weaknesses that may hinder our offering to the customer? (**Points of competitive weakness**)

Be honest about what points qualify for what label. Is having the best widget in the industry **a point of uniqueness**? Of course not; it might be an advantage, but only if you can prove it and if the quality of being the "best" is of value to the customer. You may in fact be in a commodity business in which being the "best" is hindering your price competitiveness and thus produces a competitive weakness. The power behind the grid is that you can eventually reposition most of your weaknesses as advantages if you can define the right markets and resulting customer value.

Many companies claim to have a host of **unique advantages**, but in reality, unique advantages of a product or service are rare. There are combinations of points that can make for a unique package, but it is important to use the words *unique* and *only* accurately. When a company does have a genuine competitive uniqueness it can become the holy grail of closing business. When you've appropriately questioned prospects for their needs and a prospect has expressed a dollar value for your unique offering, and that value exceeds your incremental price...game over; the prospect cannot negotiate on price and you have the sale. The problem is that too many sales reps spill their areas of uniqueness and advantages up front and a willing buyer plays coy for the sake of negotiation. The key is building tools that get your team to question first, and present relevant positioning points when appropriate.

Advantages are most powerful when you not only confirm the need but also have incontrovertible proof of your advantage's reality and value. Again, many companies are overly optimistic about what offerings of theirs are advantages in the eyes of the customer. The more honest you are in this phase the easier it will be when you engage customers in filling out the grid.

Points of **competitive equality** are important to make note of and can have a strategic benefit in sales and marketing efforts. Calling out an equality can help to neutralize the selling and marketing efforts of less savvy competitors that are touting them as advantages. This tactic brings more attention to your true and provable points of advantage.

The "downgrading technique" can also be an effective sales and marketing tactic, which you can use if you know your grid points. This is where you will strategically choose to take an advantage or even uniqueness and downgrade it to an equality. In one instance we had a client that had a unique money-back guarantee in a high-dollar software industry. Competitors lied outright, saying that they had a similar guarantee, but we couldn't call them out on it without losing credibility. Instead we created a tactic of explaining to prospects in the final phases of the decision-making process that "all good competitors have a no-risk implementation guarantee, and you will know that you have the right competitors in the final rounds by the fact that they have pointed out this specific clause in their contract. Here is ours. Again we see this as a competitive equality that probably everyone making it to this final round will clearly show in their presentation...." When those words were uttered you could just read the eyes in the room that we had struck a blow. The closing ratios of that client shot through the roof.

Points of **competitive weakness** can often be repositioned as *chosen* weaknesses that actually highlight the competitive advantage of your offering. For example, you may have the highest price—this is something that you will want to allude to early and often in selling and marketing efforts, but reposition it with the fact that the higher price enables greater R&D, service levels, and quality, which accounts not just for the difference in price but the entire investment within so many months, verses the competition, which actually has a much higher cost of ownership throughout the lifetime of the relationship.

There is power in confessing weaknesses up front and repositioning them as necessary. It tends to build credibility in your marketing and sales communication. During a turnaround there are bound to be weaknesses that need to be confessed and repositioned. The grid helps to keep communications focused and effective, and also shows customers that you are not hiding the facts, but rather are offering a more informed and competitively advantageous decision.

After you have created a Version 1 of the Positioning Points Grid with your team, use the depth interview process to involve your customers and gather their input.

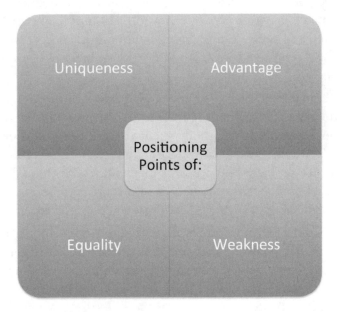

Awareness of positioning points helps in the clarification of strategy and improving the effectiveness of marketing and sales efforts.

Behind every positioning point we recommend you build these bullets:

- ✓ Benefits
- ✓ Dollarized value
- ✓ Proofs

You can begin your first versions of the grid with guesses as to the benefits, dollarized value, and proofs behind each positioning point; you will be filling these points in eventually with the results of research and your depth interviews. The benefits bullets help to keep your sales and marketing efforts focus on the results that customers buy. Customers want a job accomplished with your solution, and yet we can get too caught up in the facts about the hammer, as opposed to how well it helps to hang pictures or lay a roof.

Ultimately what can be the most persuasive messaging and positioning effort is capturing and proving the incremental value—or, more specifically, the profit—that you can bring to your customer's bottom line. When your team can effectively get customer buy-in to the incremental profits they will realize through your points of competitive uniqueness or advantage, you can effectively demand higher pricing, and you will have the advantage.

The most effective proofs are testimonials. Testimonials have the most impact when they are short, benefits-focused, and include the customer's perception of the dollars they gained because of buying from you. We help clients get these testimonials through the depth interview process. Testimonials have even more impact when photos of the customer—and, ideally, even phone numbers—are included. Being that the use of testimonials has become so prevalent and some are not legitimate, putting the phone number or other contact info gives the ultimate credibility to the testimonial.

Creating your Positioning Points Grid will build your team's competitive awareness. When these positioning points are discussed, your team will not only be more focused, but also more effective at communicating your difference in the marketplace during their marketing, qualification, and closing efforts. The document should be reviewed and updated quarterly in conjunction with your depth interview process and other steps in the strategy process. Eventually your top management will use the Positioning Points Grid as you make strategic decisions about your targeted market standing and share, as well as other key objectives we discussed in Chapter 3.

Capture New Customer Share With Face-to-Face C-Level Interviews

You may be in a situation such that hiring a third party to facilitate the depth interview process is not currently feasible. In that case, you may choose from several internal positions for this effort. In addition to the qualifications mentioned earlier you will want to look at the following considerations.

Customers will tend to open up more with higher-level authorities within your company. Whereas there are always exceptions, usually the COO will garner more information and be more objective than a VP of sales. Even members of some boards of directors or advisors could be a good substitute for a third party. Ideally the president, CEO, or owners make for excellent facilitators of a certain number of the depth interviews. The titular head of a company has an uncanny ability to bond with, impress, and open up the communication with a company's best customers.

I have coached many a president and owner on the questioning and depth interview process with great success. But even when a company is using a third party for depth interviews, I exhort the top management to consistently be a part of a minimum number of customer depth interviews. It is far too easy for customer relationships to become overly comfortable, and wrong assumptions can mount up on both sides. The depth interview process not only increases your team's competitive awareness, but it also captures untapped sales potentials and increases your customer retention.

Just as conducting the right depth interviews with the right customers has helped so many others, this process could help you to find untapped billions within your customer base.

Chapter 7
Growth-Oriented Targeting

Ensure Your Team Is Focused on the Best New Growth Potentials

For all the money wasted on sales training, if just one tenth of those resources were invested in refining the targets of the team, a multifold return would ensue. In over 20 years of facilitating sales strategy and sales innovation sessions, I've found that the top two areas sales reps will identify as what they most need to improve are productivity and the quality of their targeting—the latter of which gets them a far greater return on their investment. Most individual sales reps know that they could improve the quality of prospects on whom they are calling, yet management and marketing are usually doing little to help them refine their target lists. No more. Quarterly review of your priority targets—or "prospects" in many teams' vernacular—is a strategically valuable investment for accelerated growth, and especially in a turnaround.

In a turnaround effort improving the quality of the prospects and customers on whom you focus can often be one of the highest return efforts that you can pursue. If you take the 80/20 rule and apply it to existing customers, telling your sales and marketing team to only focus on selling the top 20 percent of customers, would it improve your results? That is an extreme example, but I have often seen that to be the wise path in a turnaround. "Firing" the bottom 20, 50, or even 80 percent of the current prospect list and only focusing on the top 20 percent can have a very profitable result. I don't know if these tactics would have the same benefit in your situation, but it proves the point on the leverage you can have in accelerating the growth of revenues and profits with this area of focus.

Having your teams and sales producers create target lists with what they believe to be their most significant and likely growth potentials, along with the process of auditing those lists, can be a powerful agent to take focus away from farming old, worn accounts and markets, and instead focus on increasing the time invested with much greater growth potentials. A common problem is "trap line fishing," which is the sales rep's habit of calling on the older, more familiar customers, because they are the ones with whom the rep is most comfortable—not necessarily the ones most likely to deliver the most new business.

I have seen cases in which changing the commission structure to more heavily weight new customer sales as opposed to existing customers is the perfect lever for accelerating growth, yet, in other situations, mining existing customers for more of their potential dollar *can* be the more effective focus. This is just one of many areas you must discern in the process of targeting.

Customer and Market Segmentation

It can be hard enough for your sales reps to look at their long list of prospective markets or customers and rank them in the most appropriate priority. Then, to be able to give the highest-priority opportunities the appropriate time and attention without any prioritization tool or list is nearly impossible. Here is a simple method for customer and prospect prioritization that sales management and marketing leadership can use with their teams on a regular basis. This tool can create a prioritized target list with uncanny accuracy that will increase the focus within the business, and the marketing and sales efforts. It helps align resources and efforts for more effective marketing and selling efforts. Although there are far more sophisticated methodologies, algorithms, and software, this is meant to be a more of a guerilla marketing tool that you can quickly build and manage yourself.

An initial step of segmenting your target prospects and top customer growth opportunities requires listing out what is important. For example, typical segmentation worksheets might include any combination of the following (and much more):

✓ Current or potential gross revenues from this customer or prospect.

✓ Current or potential gross profits (profit margin percentage).

✓ The estimated time it will take to sell this prospect/ customer this targeted amount of new revenue (the sales cycle).

✓ Percent likelihood that you will get the business.

✓ Likelihood of keeping the business over *x* number of years (retention).

✓ Spinoff, referral, or marquis value.

After deciding what is important to measure, the next step is to create a scale in each area that can be easily estimated and is in appropriate balance of priority with the other areas. You don't want one area of measure to unduly outweigh another area of measure. For example, one new customer that has gross sales of $1 million with a profit potential of $50,000 must have an appropriate measure/balance with another new customer that has gross sales of $500,000 and profitability of $100,000.

To kick off the simplest of segmentation exercises, one approach is to build a spreadsheet that lists some of the most important areas for measure. For the purpose of this exercise we'll use:

1. Revenue.

2. Profit.

3. Percent likelihood of getting the sale.

Make a list of prospects and put these three columns next to each one. In order to quantify things like gross revenues and percent likelihood of winning the business, you must create a scale. In the following example, we will use a 1 to 10 scale for each column with these formulas:

✓ 1 point for each $50,000 of gross revenue.

✓ 1 point for each $5,000 of profits.

✓ 1 point for every 10 percent in our estimate of percent likelihood of winning the business—if we have a 50/50 chance of winning this business it will get a 5; if it is a "done deal" because it's our brother, then it will get a 10.

Make your estimates, fill in your chart, and then add up your numbers in a Total Value / Priority column. Your prioritized list will look like this:

	Prospect	Gross Revenue	1-10 Scale for Revenue	Profits	1-10 Scale for Profits	Percent Likelihood of Winning the Business 1=10% 10=100%	Total Value Priority
1							
2	Schem Software	$250,000	5	$35,000	7	7	19
3	Leasing Associates	$300,000	6	$30,000	6	5	17
4	G. Martin & Company	$500,000	10	$10,000	2	2	14
5	Daniels & Calds	$100,000	2	$10,000	2	9	13
6	SolutionIndex	$50,000	1	$5,000	1	5	7
7							

Upon further analysis you may realize that gross revenues are not nearly as high a priority, and thus you may experiment with lowering the 1–10 scale by only giving 1 point for every $100,000 of gross revenues. Play with the scales until you know that your prioritized list is pretty much on target.

We recommend starting by segmenting existing customers so that you'll have a history of real numbers, not just estimates, and you'll likely be able to find untapped sales potential as well. Afterward do a similar effort with prospects.

The bottom line is, once you have segmentation worksheets created, you'll find a much more focused, prioritized, and profitable direction for selling and marketing efforts. I have seen this one simple tool increase revenues and profits by seven figures for small eight-figure companies. If you aren't facilitating customer segmentation, you must begin to immediately.

Knowing Who Your Ideal Customers Are

We used the customer segmentation tool to focus on prospective new business, but a similar exercise must be done with existing customers. It is best to start all segmentation efforts by determining who your best and most profitable customers currently are. Most companies do a poor job of prioritizing their most profitable customers; as a result, they do an even poorer job of prioritizing their prospective customers, and thus are losing growth potential.

Can your management, marketing, sales, and service teams clarify the priority of your customers? If not, why? The root of this problem goes back to the poor communication between these various facets of the business. Those who may know the profitability of a customer or of profit-draining issues with certain types of customers are often not communicating that valuable information to the other areas.

As much as possible, management must determine what makes a profitable customer. There are as many variances of costs as there are businesses, but you can start with the financial information on the books with regard to profit margin percentages, total profits per customer, and customer types. Your challenge is to uncover the soft costs that may also be affecting profits, and merge and balance this information with the harder financial information.

Conduct interviews and hold meetings with key representatives from sales, service, and any other areas that might have relevant information about the soft costs behind specific customers and types. Ask your team who they believe are your most profitable and least profitable specific customers and customer types, and why.

For example, a certain type of larger customer that is paying higher margins than average may be thought of as the highest-priority type of customer, but in reality your service reps may be spending more unpaid time with those customers per unit installed than any other customer type. Thus, what you thought was one of your best customers may be only marginally profitable or even unprofitable.

From the information you have garnered, create a customer segmentation worksheet for existing customers based on the true net profitability, considering the hard and soft costs of your various customers.

Typically this soft information isn't secret, but it is rarely gathered and discussed on a regular basis. Even rarer is having it worked into some sort of customer segmentation tool that is shared throughout the team to make clear just who are your best and most profitable customers. The benefits of this exercise are that your best customers will be retained longer, your worst customers can pay the price increases needed or be fired (or even strategically handed over to your competition), and your marketing and sales efforts will be more adroitly aimed at the highest-profit customer types.

Leveraging the Targeting Process to Increase Sales and Effectiveness With the Three-20s Tactic

Management, marketing, and sales producers should have what I call the "Three 20s" at their side at all times:

1. Top 20 prospects.

2. Top 20 customers.

3. Top 20 advocates.

In some situations the number may need to be much higher or lower, but the point is that each list has a lot of opportunity in it that is usually ripe for mining. The tactic is simple: have individuals, units, and your company as a whole create a top 20 list of customers, advocates, and prospects. The benefits of having these lists in front of each group are as follows:

✓ **Top customers** will be better serviced and cross-sold for additional business. They will also be better mined for testimonials and referrals or connections that will lead to additional business.

✓ **Top advocates** will be met with or at least talked with on a regular basis. To be an advocate they must be a connector to new business and a supporter/champion/advocate of your company. In many cases we have had sales teams set the objective of meeting with a minimum of eight advocates per month for the sake of asking for connections to new business. We charted the results and found that these "sales calls" are more productive and profitable than many other types of prospecting and selling calls as the selling cycle on these connections is usually much shorter.

✓ **Top prospect** lists have several uses and benefits. For one thing, they keep your sales reps focused on the top new customer opportunities. Also, these lists can be used in the most effective referral gathering strategy that we have found—it's called **The Echeloned Targets Referral Strategy**.

The strategy is to have every sales rep carry with him or her copies of the top 20 prospects (or potentially as many as 60) on an 8.5-by-11 sheet of paper, and set the objective of showing it to a minimum number of people each week or month. The paper can contain three things; a long list of specific company names, a list of specific notable people, and then a few bullets of your ideal prospect types or profile points.

Then the goal is for the sales rep to pull out the list at the appropriate time during a meeting and simply ask, "Do you know or have any familiarity with anyone on this list?" Then he or she would just listen and check off those they mention, and note relevant comments. The sales rep then has the ability to reference this connection during initial calls to those prospects. Having a connection in a prospecting effort has been proven to greatly increase the chance of progress and a sale. Of course, one of the first places to take this list is to the 20 advocates and perhaps even the 20 customers on the other top 20 lists. This is a far superior strategy to just asking for referrals, and is something that management and marketing may be able to help sales manage through the Three-20s strategy.

How to Foster Balance Between Short-Term and Long-Term Business

Many companies and individual sales producers get caught at one time or another with not enough business closing in the short term, or not enough business lined up for the long term (business not set to close in 90 days or more is commonly "long-term," and 90 days or less is short-term for many companies). Here is a simple process and tool that will help to balance the focus of the sales and marketing teams as well as empower management to better coach and provide support for sales producers.

Create a simple spreadsheet with the appropriate room and slots to capture the top accounts most likely to close in the next 90 days, and perhaps even include a space for target date. Likewise, include a parallel list for accounts that are actively being marketed, met with, sold, courted, and so on, but aren't expected to close for more than 90 days.

Once sales reps create the two lists it usually becomes apparent that there is a shortage in either their long-term or short-term pipeline. This is an important but often overlooked area for sales managers.

One of the most important questions for sales managers to ask comes after sales reps tell you what date an account is expected to close. Simply ask, "Why do you think that is when you will be able to sign on this account?" The quality of the answer indicates the quality of the selling process and awareness of that account.

This tool also helps sales and marketing to better align efforts with one another, thus increasing closing ratios and even sales call productivity. Keeping the pipeline properly balanced can mean the difference between solvency and bankruptcy.

Chapter 8
Growth Through Innovations in Marketing

Synergizing and Echeloning Your Marketing and Sales Teams

All too often there is a wall of separation between marketing and sales departments, and that wall can frequently be a root cause of a company's failing performance. While facilitating turnarounds and gearing up for an accelerated growth mode, you must destroy that wall and bring these two groups as closely together as possible. Stories abound of marketing efforts that the sales team abhors and rebel against embracing. "They have no idea what we need in sales" is a common lamentation. And marketing departments often challenge, "Just what do they do all day, and why don't those idiots follow up on these qualified leads we've paid good money for?"

Whether communication is acrimonious or there's none at all, you are in a fight for the life and growth of the company. Wake your teams up to that fact and take them through the tools discussed in Chapters 1, 2, and 3. Have them set objectives they must work on together. Demand that they become a cohesive and symbiotic team. You must require them to aggressively innovate ways to work together on helping to turn the company around and quickly increase revenues and profits. If they aren't working together, point out that they are in violation of the growth values that the entire team has contributed to and agreed upon together.

If they aren't working together they are probably ignoring key growth objectives that have been set and agreed upon.

There is no room for this wall between marketing and sales; it will kill your company. Together, more than anyone in your company, these departments can bring in the cash flow to keep you afloat. Buy a "Join or Die" revolutionary flag and hang it in their departments to make the point.

There are many projects on which your marketing and sales teams could work together, but innovating the next prospecting tools and ideas that give sales a new "purpose for a sales call" can have an immediate impact on production.

Marketing Drip Strategies That Soften Aggressive Sales Landings

Sales teams are invigorated when new and different marketing tactics are used to help break through to specific new customers, or to open further doors with existing customers. As with most efforts it is important that you have the sales and marketing teams work together in the marketing innovation process.

Now that you've created the "Top 20" list of prospective customers I spoke of in Chapter 7, it's time to put it to work. A powerful step in marketing is to test and continuously improve marketing drip strategies. Typically, the best marketing drip strategies involve sending three or more targeted marketing pieces to a prospect for the purpose of setting a selling appointment or making a sale. The pieces are usually spaced five to 10 days apart, and they all share a common theme—similar colors, logos, photography, and messages that improve the mnemonic impact. What makes these drip strategies effective is that, unlike a singular mailing or effort, the series tends to have a synergistic impact and avoids the trap of the one-hit-wonder. For some industries the percentage of appointments set (as well as closing ratios) can greatly increase when targets receive marketing such as this that has "softened the beaches."

I'm not recommending any of the following strategies specifically, but I share them to illustrate the power a little creativity can have in turning around a sales team's production and effectiveness.

Cartoon Humor Opened the Door

One of the larger insurance companies conducted a test with 10,000 qualified prospects who were owners of small, privately held companies. A creative letter with a customized cartoon was sent. The letter was a benefits-only brief missive extolling the financial benefits one of the insurance agents would be able to bring the prospect in just one or two short meetings. The cartoons were reproductions of work drawn by a nationally recognized cartoonist. The cartoons were merely customized in the printing with the name of the owner and his or her company, and were framed in an inexpensive but classy frame that could be hung up or set on a desk. The mailings were followed up by well-scripted phone calls and an additional incentive to meet with the agent. The end result? The company set appointments with more than 90 percent of the targeted prospects.

The Train Rode In

A marketing firm mailed five packages of high-end display train cars to presidents of mid-sized companies who were well-qualified targets for the firm's services. Creative notes accompanied each package and gift. The final package was empty but felt weighty, as it was a wooden box that was supposed to house the engine car of the train set. The note simply said, "If you would like to meet with the company that could be the engine to growing your sales, please let us know if you would share a few minutes of your time when we call next week. We also will bring you the engine of this model set as a thank-you, regardless of whether we engage in business or not." The firm secured appointments with more than 90 percent of the prospects, and sold the majority of them on their services.

The Ace of Spades

Two young sales reps had been assigned to work together on specific larger and harder-to-win accounts. They were having a tough time getting through to some of the plant managers who were the largest of these prospects. Through the innovation process they came up with a host of ideas and decided on one that involved sending an envelope with nothing more than a playing card in it. The first card to arrive was a jack of spades. Next Monday, another card arrived; it was the queen of spades, followed by a king of spades a week later. Finally on the fourth Monday, the sales reps themselves showed up. As a way of introduction, they told the secretary at the front desk to "tell the plant manager that the Ace of Spades is here to meet him." A 100-watt smile flashed across the secretary's face as she called the plant manager saying, "The Ace of Spades is here!" Shortly thereafter, the manager arrived and greeted the sales reps with a hearty laugh and an ebullient handshake. All had a fun time, and these prospects went on a fast track to becoming a customer.

A/B Test

As with many marketing promotion efforts, you should "A/B" test as appropriate. A/B testing is the simple step of pitting your two best ideas against each other in a promotion to see which draws the greatest response or facilitates the best results. Between an aggressive innovation effort geared toward getting the sales team in front of more high-priority prospects and a more echeloned effort among sales and marketing, you will be harvesting some healthy growth in short order.

Getting Testimonials

When a company is on the ropes, this is a powerful turn-around tool for bringing back confidence to the team and finding some new business—and it works just as well with a healthy company. Getting testimonial letters from successful customer relationships has multiple benefits:

- ✓ It is a powerful process to build your sales reps' and your overall team's faith and confidence in the company and product. Too often reps begin to believe the logic of customers lost to the competition.

- ✓ The letters from customers build the stickiness of the relationship and serve as a solidification tool for increased retention.

- ✓ The letters provide a powerful arsenal of credibility for your use with prospective customers.

Here is how to get and use these letters and quotes for increasing sales and selling effectiveness. My company has many dozens of powerful testimonial letters in our files. I rhetorically ask clients I'm coaching on this issue, "You know why they are such excellent testimonial letters? ...Because I wrote them!" Here is the point, and a key step in the process: Your team must take a full accounting of all the specific benefits, impact, and dollarized value your solutions have brought (or are tracking to bring) to your customer. Then your team must write the first draft of the ideal letter.

Most customers, especially your economic buyer, are not fully aware of all you have done for them; all of the impact and value you have brought to them. Although they have made the decision to invest in your company and they have probably received enough evidence that you are a good investment for them, you can't assume the best and take a rest. You are missing the boat if you allow them to remain ignorant of your full value. What you must have your team do is write out the ideal testimonial letter with bulleted items of benefit, and ideally a dollarized value of impact written into the letter as if your customers wrote it themselves. Then you are going to ask your customers to put it on their letterhead and give you a copy.

Customers will inevitably augment and actually improve most of the testimonial letters because there will be some things you weren't aware of in regard to what they value. When we present our drafts of testimonial letters to customers we have a note above the bullets section asking the question, "Is there anything else that you value in the relationship, or any other benefit you have experienced that we haven't listed here?" Invariably both parties are learning new things about the full value of the relationship.

I have seen countless examples of economic buyers/decision-makers at my client's customer companies that were aware of less than half of the full value my client was delivering. When we crafted testimonial letters and gathered the supporting evidence to show, in many examples, where there had been incontrovertible seven-, even eight-figure impact on these customers' companies, we locked those customers in for life. I have heard many cases of the buyer saying something akin to, "We were just about to shop out your services and look for a better deal, but after seeing just how impactful you have been at our company, not only are you getting me to put that testimonial letter on our letterhead, but I want to lock in our relationship for the next three years!"

Get New Business

Set an objective with your sales team and perhaps involve marketing in getting a minimum number of testimonial letters approved in the first few months. In the case of a turnaround, target existing customers that have the most untapped additional business potential. Measure how much more business you are able to win after using this tactic and you will permanently add this process into your arsenal of selling tools.

Increase Morale

Regarding teams that have lost their faith and confidence in a product or company, I have found that between the laudatory testimonial quotes that we gather in our depth interview process and the testimonial letters, any team's confidence can be turned around, which in turn leads to the company's turnaround.

Focus on Value Instead of Pricing

With clients in business-to-business environments, after my depth interviews have been completed, I particularly enjoy asking the team, "What do you think we really sell? What is it that our customers buy from us? I have talked to our customers and I have learned something. We don't sell products. We don't sell service. We don't sell relationship. We sell profit!" When you ask customers enough of the right questions and drill down to the root of what they value and why they make one choice over the other, what is the ultimate result and what is the value? It is profitability, or, put another way, "we just make more money with your client," that I consistently hear.

Positioning your relationships with a focus on increasing customers' profit helps to make price irrelevant and total overall cost (TOC) the focus. I have seen great success with clients when this becomes a stated goal and actually becomes part of their literal mission, and then marketing and sales positioning, to ultimately create a very powerful proposition. Most businesses have this opportunity, but are afraid to explore with their customers just how much their solutions are worth to them. Discovering, with as much specificity as you can, just how much profit your company can incrementally deliver over the competition, is one of the most valuable insights you must uncover.

Companies—especially those with mediocre sales producers—frequently believe that it is their higher pricing that is restricting their sales. Often this misunderstanding exists while competitors have a higher pricing strategy and thus are more profitable. With the use of the depth interview process and testimonial letter process, you will soon become more and more confident about the incremental profits your company helps to deliver. Having a higher price is usually a strategically good thing, and even an advantage in marketing, positioning, and selling effectiveness. Your challenge in the turnaround of the team is to thoroughly educate them on the full value that your solution delivers to the well-targeted existing and prospective customers.

A Goal of Marketing

The ideal marketing process is one that is so thoroughly effective that it makes any sales process or effort superfluous. A company will often either be forced to pay for more effective marketing or for more effective selling. Ideally you are on a path of continuous improvement in your marketing so that sales become easier and easier as time goes on. If this is not the case, then you must begin to implement the innovation process as a permanent part of your marketing efforts.

Chapter 9
Increasing Sales Productivity

Productivity Improvement Is Not the Panacea

Although productivity is commonly noted by management and sales reps as an initial area they want to improve, I'm not as enthusiastic about focusing on this area. Firstly, there is only so far that the needle can be moved with regard to productivity. Although we can facilitate improvements in this area it's usually not the root of a turnaround issue, nor is it the lowest-hanging fruit for improving profitability and growth. Secondly, and more importantly, the return on increased productivity is usually not as great as the return on an increased focus on higher-priority business, optimization of positioning, pricing, value, and other areas, which will more quickly and more easily garner much higher returns in profit and growth. Nevertheless, there are a few strategies that can quickly bring about increases in productivity as well as accelerate the rate of innovation that will also help to increase productivity and effectiveness. Ultimately these efforts do have enough impact on the bottom line that they are worth the attention.

Wielding Your Strategic Abandonment Sword

For all that has been written about time management, the fact is that you really can't manage time. You can manage priorities. This is why having a foundational strategy, clarifying key objectives, identifying critical success factor activities, and implementing continuous improvement through an innovation process will have the most impact on effectiveness. I think it is worth reviewing the misnomer of "time management" with your team.

As you discuss productivity and direction with your team you will want to ask the two most important priority-management questions that help you align your team's direction and enable them to fall into echelon as a team. One of those questions is, "What is the most important thing for me/you/us to be working on now?" The more important but less frequently asked question is, "What do I/you/we need to stop doing?" It is only through regularly asking this question of yourself and your team that you will begin to optimize focus and productivity. In a turnaround it is critical that you thoroughly look at these strategic abandonment opportunities on a macro and micro basis. With all of the innovations, changes, and new initiatives that you will be required to undertake, you must also be abandoning practices to allow for the time to focus on these higher priorities.

Echeloned Quiet Hours

The "Quiet Hour" is a powerful productivity improvement practice that some companies have made part of their culture. It can greatly improve your team's ability to focus more time on the turnaround and growth strategy. One of the greatest challenges for any knowledge worker, let alone sales, is the ability to spend enough time on non-urgent but highly important work.

How often are your employees working under the "tyranny of the urgent," jumping from one small, urgent, but unimportant fire to the next, reassuring themselves that they are doing important work because "at least the forest isn't ablaze!"? The problem is, their important but not urgent work is to cut wood. Many of the critical success factor activities you will identify under each of your objectives will fall under this category of non-urgent but important.

The steps to implement the quiet hour are simple. You block off time on your calendar as if it is an appointment with yourself. You close the door—literally or figuratively. You have phones forwarded to voice mail, with a message that gives the caller a way to get through to you if it is urgent, and says at what time you'll be available. (This enables others to call you back rather than leaving another message.) Lastly you turn off the e-mail alarm that rings with every spam that hits your mailbox. Now you are ready to work with uninterrupted focus for 60 minutes (or whatever amount of time you choose).

For management, the quiet hours are the ideal time to focus on the critical success factor activities that are tied to your strategic growth objectives. You should aim to have a minimum number of quiet hours per week for such work. Quiet hours work because we benefit from uninterrupted focus. You will notice that you will pick up an increased momentum. The practice almost seems illogical during a turnaround mode, but the fact is, in such a time of stress, you and your team need to slow down to speed up; you need the quiet and solidity of an hour to knock out important work.

Sales reps often have a terrible challenge in getting enough time to set appointments. My recommendation to sales managers is to encourage or require the team to habitually have a minimum number of hours blocked every week for such work. An approach that works for some teams is to have predetermined hours around which the entire sales team goes into quiet hour for the purpose of appointment-setting. This is an activity that is often put off, so any little tool to help maintain a habit of more calls can help.

If you aren't satisfied with the amount of time dedicated to non-urgent but highly important work on your calendar and your team's calendar, and if you want to ensure that more focus is given to the critical success factor activities associated with your growth or turnaround objectives, consider instituting this as a company-wide practice so that it becomes an Echeloned Quiet Hour.

Blocking off Focus Hours on your calendar for strategic non-urgent growth and turnaround work ensures that more non-urgent high-priority work gets done. Treat these hours like you have clocked into the production line to ensure zero interruptions. Strategic plans become useless unless the required work hits someone's calendar or to-do list.

Using Priority Management to Accomplish the Turnaround Strategy

Your turnaround strategy will beget thousands of necessary actions that need to be taken. It is paramount that these actions happen as soon as possible, and in the right order. Thus it is not overkill to ensure that your team is prioritizing activities with expeditiousness and aplomb. When the following practice becomes part of a company's culture and vernacular, it also becomes part of the foundation for a highly intensified focus and productivity.

Knowing Your "A"s & "B"s and 1-2-3s

These three steps have three key benefits: First, you'll get more done. Some say this approach will "save" more than an hour a day, but in reality it just means you have accomplished one more hour of work from your to-do list than you otherwise would have. Secondly, you'll be less stressed. Knowing your plan, and knowing things aren't falling through the cracks, gives you a greater sense of control and ease. You'll wake up to a purpose, not an alarm clock. Thirdly, you'll save money. There will be less overnight mail and last-minute rushes that cost you time and money. Finally, and most importantly, you'll get more of the most important work done first. That is a heck of a list of benefits for what can take as little as five minutes a day.

Have you ever noticed the way every time-management guru seems to push his or her own custom labels for to-do lists? At first it was the A, B, C, and Ds, and you had to know what each letter meant, but nobody remembered, so they would print it on their custom day-planning sheets...and then you would forget to use them and just create a list of to-dos on your overpriced calendar.

In reality there are only two types of priorities that you need to be aware of in daily planning: urgent and non-urgent. Anything that is due today is an urgent matter and thus an "A" priority. If you would be forced to work late if a certain task wasn't accomplished by quitting time, then it is an A.

If you have a lot of "A"s rolling over to another day, you aren't being honest about your priorities. So if anything could roll over to tomorrow's list, no matter how important, it is still just a B. Every day is full of interruptions that will change your originally planned course, and there will be times when you must decide if you can "stop everything" to answer someone else's urgent request. For example, if it is 2 p.m. and someone comes in with an urgent need that will tie up your time for the rest of the day, yet you still have a couple of "A"s on the list, you must make the decision that you'll either be working late or will need to make a few phone calls to see if the "A"s can wait. Having the must-be-done-todays clearly marked gives you the ability to decide upon changes with greater alacrity. It also gives you an out when people attempt to tie up your day with inappropriate urgencies.

The most important step in your daily planning is numbering your "B"s. "A"s will always be addressed because they are "A"s. You will still want to number "A"s and work through them in priority, in case there is a redirection of your day, but thanks to this practice none of your "A"s will fall through the cracks. The difference between mediocre workers and highly effective workers is that the highly effective get much more high-priority work done sooner, regardless of its urgency. In other words, they get the 1-2-3s of their B list done first. Whether you have a knack for working on the right thing at the right time, or if you need to better plan the course of your activities, you will optimize your focus and save time with the simple act of numbering. The average to-do list has more than 30 hours of work on it and is a great source of stress and delay. By mid-week you will be nowhere near half finished with it, and too often will begin flipping around the pages of all these to-dos, not looking for the next highest priority, but rather the fastest, easiest thing to do next, just to have the satisfaction of crossing off an item on the list.

Plan your priorities the night before. If you wait until the morning, interruptions and distractions are likely to occur, and before you know it, you will be halfway through your day. But at the end of the day, you will be more realistic and aware, with tasks fresh in your mind, knowing what are the highest priorities. You will also want to create a list of only enough to-dos for the next day—the rest can be listed somewhere else. There is a sense of ease and satisfaction to be gained from working on a list that is likely to be accomplished in one day. For instance, I was once interviewing a president of a large hotel chain, and after I asked him what was the most important advice he had ever received, he said, "It was to create a list of only six items a day, to prioritize it, and to work through it in priority every day. It changed my life and it is why I'm in this position today."

The way in which this president related his advice was similar to a classic old story about the first CEO to have earned $1 million a year. He brought in the highest-profile consultant of the day for a long consulting project with the objective of increasing productivity. Although the CEO expected a long engagement with a big fee attached, the consultant stopped the engagement after trying to work with the CEO for two days. He said, "My work here is done; I have just one piece of advice for you. Are you ready to take notes?" The CEO was infuriated, as he felt he was being fired; he had promised his board of directors significant progress from this engagement and now he was about to get a "little piece of advice"? The consultant said, "Just write these three things down. First, make a list of just the six most important things to do for the day. Second, number it in priority. Third, work through it in priority, and if a fire comes up—literally or figuratively—in your plant, put it out, but come right back to where you left off." The CEO seethed and asked what the consultant expected to be paid for this little piece of advice. The consultant quipped back, "Nothing, until you have done it for 28 days. Then just send me a check for whatever you think it was worth." A short 28 days later the CEO sent a check for more than $20,000—a considerable sum for the 1920s when this occurred.

Consider how you might roll out the practices of an Echeloned Quite Hour and the A-B-Cs and 1-2-3s throughout your team. I have found that when we make this part of the strategic growth planning process or a turnaround it has a significant impact on follow-through and progress toward the quarterly milestones.

Remember, the best laid plans are fruitless unless the work needed to accomplish them hits the calendar.

Stretch Days, Weeks, or Months Can Increase Productivity

Most sales producers have a paradigm set for how many selling calls they can make in a week, but it is often far from their potential. One way to shatter those misconceptions is for every sales producer to attempt one "stretch day" or week each quarter—a day or week when they present to as many prospects as humanly possible. What will result is a host of innovations on how to improve productivity and increase sales.

Determine the appropriate length of time. The benefit of an entire week is that if sales reps go that long at a much higher level of productivity, they are likely to see how much closer their regular weeks could come to this stretch level of productivity. For example, in one industry with a client we've worked with for many years, I knew that the more productive reps could see as many as 15 appointments per week with no problem. The perception though with most reps was that eight to 10 appointments would be a "good week," and the average for many was just five appointments a week. This doesn't sound like very many, but in this company's high-ticket industry where seven-figure incomes were possible and middle six–figure sales rep incomes are common, reps could get away with low productivity and still be "surviving" with enough commissions.

I would first challenge the reps at each location to consider what they thought to be the absolute maximum number of appointments they could see in a stretch week. The reps answered 12 to 15. I then challenged them with the idea that if they had two or more weeks to prepare for the stretch week, and if they aimed to book five breakfasts, five lunches, and five cocktail hours, that would be 15, and they would still have the hours of 9 a.m. to noon and 2 p.m. to 5 p.m. to schedule even more appointments. "Couldn't you fit at least another 10 in those slots, if not 20?" I asked. After that, with the help of a creative competition, incentives, and the offloading of some low-priority work, it was common for many reps to see 20 to 25 appointments during their stretch week. These are not numbers we expected them to maintain, but in every case the stretch experience had been done and they could never go back to the same paradigm. More importantly, they would maintain an increased level of productivity throughout their career.

In another instance the sales reps were only able to have one stretch day, and only one rep at a time could be attempting a stretch day because others were needed to cover potential service calls. The average productivity at this company was only five selling calls per week. Their selling calls could be very short, so this was abysmal. They had allowed many different areas to distract them from selling activity, so they instituted an intense innovation effort geared toward eliminating, delegating, improving, and dynamically changing things. They no longer had to fill out detailed call reports by hand; rather, just after ending each appointment, they would call in the details to a voice mail system for an office manager to transcribe. They began using street mapping software in conjunction with their contact database to prevent crisscrossing their large territories and getting lost on unfamiliar roads, and this reduced windshield time. They offloaded certain service calls and phone calls that were unnecessarily being routed to them, and much more. As a result, during just one focus day, they were able to achieve as many as 20 quality-selling calls that led to follow-up sales-related activity and ultimately a bid. This shockingly high one-day potential transformed both their mindset and their systems so that they were able to measurably increase weekly productivity. As a result, that location went from worst to first in its region. It wasn't so much a focus on productivity as the innovation process that turned around the team.

Here are some points to remember as you facilitate your own stretch process:

✓ Begin with a focus on the innovation process. Emphasize that it's not the people that are broken but the process. Remind them of the urgency of your situation and the strategic growth objectives.

✓ Share with the team the current best practices and the productivity levels of your most productive reps.

✓ Challenge your team regarding what they think is the maximum possible number of calls.

✓ Create competition, incentives, and a sense of fun around the process.

✓ Give plenty of time for participants to "stack" their stretch days or week. There is nothing wrong with taking three weeks to pack a week to the max. They will end up increasing productivity on both sides of a stretch week.

✓ Implement the innovations, and pull in others to support sales in this process.

✓ Celebrate and analyze your successes so that you can scale them across the team.

✓ Consider making stretch days/weeks a regular practice, but be very careful not to conduct them too frequently. They can easily burn people out if improperly used.

Get Your Team in Front of More Prospective Customers

How important is it for your business to increase the amount of initial conversations and meetings with new prospective customers? For many businesses it is one of the higher priority critical success factors. As such it demands your creative attention and could be the key to your turnaround.

One of the greatest frustrations for a sales producer is making the calls to set appointments. Here are few tactics that can help your team make setting and seeing more appointments easier, faster, and more successful. If productivity truly is at a fraction of its potential in the sales team and one of these tactics can work, then this action alone could make the difference in turning the company around.

Setting up call campaigns as a follow-up to a particular mailing can help to ensure that the sales team will make the necessary number of calls to optimize their productivity. Working in tandem with marketing efforts, if you were to have a monthly process of a certain number of mailings going out per sales rep, and require follow-up within so many weeks of each mailing, you can create a marketing and sales rhythm, which can become a key to turning around sales forces that have gotten stuck in a rut of low call activity. You will need to ensure that the targets are well chosen and the approaches used in the process are kept fresh by engraining the innovation process throughout this effort.

Consider having pre-set times every day for appointment-setting, or having reps set appointments together in teams. Some companies have instituted teamed competitions, and just the fact that a pair of reps commit to sitting down to the phones at the same time makes a significant impact on follow-through and results. This idea has even been applied at clients that have remote sales forces: The paired teams check in just before and just after the call times and share ideas and results.

Consider using full- or part-time appointment-setters. You may even have on your staff right now the perfectly skilled people with the time to fill up the calendars of the sales team. Often you will find that detail-oriented, personable people whom you have managing the office or directing phone calls are more suited to diligently filling up the spaces of other people's calendars. These types of employees are often more strategic about how they might fill the calendar and map out the travel of your sales team. In other environments outsourcing appointment-setting is an appropriate option and can be less costly than hiring or carving out the time from your current staff.

You have to get past any complaints you might receive along the lines of "setting appointments is the sales team's job!" In fact, part of the definition of management is to leverage the strengths of the human resources on your team while minimizing the impact of their inherent weaknesses. Stop the stubborn fight of trying to get salespeople to do things they might not be as effective at doing, if that is the case in your team. Your sales team is probably effective at the actual selling, if they can just get in front of more people, so it's time for you to look at this creatively.

Innovate the appointment-setting process. Whether you are gathering ideas from the marketing side or looking at how and with whom the appointments are being set, you can usually identify areas for innovation. I recommend that you and other innovative members of the team just sit, observe, and listen to the process of appointment-setting (just as you should occasionally be doing on selling calls). After I had helped a client refine its messaging, which ultimately led to innovations in the verbiage used in appointment-setting efforts, I sat to observe the sales reps use their new, individualized scripts. In addition to seeing the new scripts lead to a significant improvement in appointment-setting ratios, the process of sitting and observing led to another important insight and innovation: I noticed that there was a common habit in the reps' delivery. When they got to the critical question of asking for the appointment they would go up in the tone of their voice, like a child who lacks confidence and is asking for permission from a parent. Upon further research I found that the child tone is subconsciously read by the listener as a lack of confidence. You might notice the way newscasters' voices always seem to go down at the end of their sentences. They are coached heavily on inflection and the tone of their voice, as these factors greatly affect their credibility. At my client's location we discovered that coaching the team on this one point raised appointment-setting ratios even further. The lesson here is that for such an important process it is critical to occasionally have a third party look closely at it and apply the innovation process for continuous improvements.

Do you believe that your sales team is paid to sell—in other words, get and keep more customers—and that everything else is secondary? Many leaders tell me emphatically that this is what they believe, but their processes indicate a much different priority. Sales reps are required—and then either punished or incentivized—to file irrelevant paperwork or gather information that is a significant drain on their time and of no use to their main purpose. Often when you take everything off of their plate except for the absolute essential activities related to their central purpose, great increases in productivity can occur.

I recommend that you install an innovation process for optimizing the amount of time that sales reps spend in front of decision-makers who can expand the business. If others can work on retention and sales can focus on expansion with a hunter-and-farmer approach, then you'll probably be able to open the funnel to a wider throughput.

Consider beginning a campaign in which a sales productivity czar looks at every piece of documentation, call reporting, note taking, and communication that might be unnecessary, and abolish the outdated and unneeded with a passion. The effort goes back to the classic questions, "What do we need to *stop* doing, and what, if we weren't doing it today, would we *not* institute as a practice if we were considering beginning it anew?

Break the Glass Ceiling of Commission Caps

CEOs are often maligned for getting large incomes and bonuses in public companies, but I believe the bigger sin is for small and mid-sized private companies to have any limit on the earning potential of the sales producers.

I can understand why larger companies who have a "promote from within" policy might need to cap out sales producers by splitting territories and or other methods—they will only find internal candidates who are willing to make that next step up in responsibility if there is some increase in pay; and without the caps, there might be no incentive to move up the ladder. That is a rare situation, however, limited mostly to the Fortune-500 companies.

Is there any sense of jealousy in you or throughout your company toward the top-echelon sales earners, who might be earning far more than any of the executives? Jealousy of this sort is often the impetus behind instituting practices that nip healthy growth in the bud, such as the capping of commissions or "re-alignments" that have the objective of bringing top sales earners' incomes "more in-line." When you are on the ropes in a turnaround, the person who gets the credit or how much the best sales producers are earning must be the least of your concerns. I have seen far too many examples when the unleashing of a few—or even just one— of the power-selling top-echelon sales performers was the key to keeping a company afloat and directed toward sustained health.

As a leader you must address the bad attitudes that might be directed either way with the top sales performers. You must also work to eliminate any possible constraining factor that could be governing your top sales producers from looking for much greener pastures. Many significant strategic innovations for a business and its direction have come when a salesperson had the financial reward (as well as the permission) for looking outside the typical business and market to exponentially larger markets. From million-dollar commissions to even billion-dollar commissions, the result has been an expansion in the economy, the company, jobs, and ultimately many families' lives, which were improved because leadership wasn't afraid to pay a sales rep handsomely for such significant innovation.

Chapter 10
Echeloning Your Sales Groups for Accelerated Growth

Team Selling Calls

The concept is simple: Team up salespeople in pairs to ride together on a percentage of sales calls. When you put some structure to this process and establish some key objectives to be met, ideas, sales results, and even productivity will increase. The chief benefit you will experience is increased sales call effectiveness. One of the biggest problems with sales teams is that they aren't cross-pollinating growth-oriented ideas that exist within the team, and thus individuals aren't continuously improving.

As you facilitate a turnaround or intensified growth effort, these teaming strategies may seem counterintuitive at first. When you are constrained with a smaller-than-desired team and your goal is to have your team talk with as many prospective customers as possible, taking half of your team "off the street" so that teams of two can ride or make phone calls together may seem to be cutting productivity in half. But the reality is that synergy and acceleration will occur when this process is well managed. Sales teaming will cost money and time, just like any training and innovation efforts, but it will have clear and profitable dividends.

You may have noticed that some industries make nearly all of their selling calls in teams of two or more. These are usually industries in which there is complex build-out of a product or service that necessitates having all of the participating parties involved throughout the selling process. In such industries I have success-fully implemented the reverse of sales teaming: The client and I mandated a small percentage of calls (mostly qualifying calls) to be made by just one person. This helped to increase productivity in the qualification phase. Still, to keep the sales cycle as short as possible in these industries, team calls worked best for most of the follow-through. So, regardless of whether your industry requires more team calling or less, you must regularly discern the optimal balance. Like many of the turnaround ideas in this book, this is about getting out of the rut and doing things differently.

The Benefits of Team Calls With Internal and External Customers

Your sales team is a group of internal customers who often get the short end of the stick as far as being served by sales manage-ment and the rest of the company. While customers on the receiv-ing end of a team call will benefit from many new ideas, insights, and motivation, so will the evaluator—whether it is a fellow sales rep or someone from management. I often hear how even the most senior of sales producers who may be sharing a great amount of wisdom, experience, and feedback on calls to their younger sales team members end up learning as much for themselves in the process.

You will also discover that recommendations tend to be more readily received because they're from a peer instead of manage-ment. Too often your sales team thinks home-office (and even sales) management "doesn't really know what it's like out there right now anyway."

One of the biggest impacts of the process is on the customer and prospects. Your external customers often only have one im-pression of your company, and it's not from your marketing col-lateral, the home-office team, or even the product, but rather the impression of your company comes from just one face: the sales rep. Customers will make judgments and associations both good and bad about your company solely because of their one key contact. Whether a prospect likes his designated sales representative better or the visiting selling partners he may occasionally meet, it's a win-win. In the first case your prospect sees that he has a person he likes as his key contact, and in the second case the customer sees that the team has even better people throughout the organization. But the bigger benefit of team calls in regard to the impression made on customers is this: Research shows that team calls build the credibility of the company and the chief individual customer contact, which ultimately leads to increased closing ratios.

The Objectives of Team Calls

Each and every sales producer should focus on and leverage his or her strengths. Often, strengths can be best leveraged and weaknesses can be most ameliorated by having a selling partner on strategically chosen calls, or involving a peer in pre-call planning. One objective is to have the selling partner evaluate the other's performance or preparation regarding particular areas. Secondly, the partner should also offer constructive criticism and specific ideas for improvement. There are many areas you can choose to focus on:

✓ Quality of targets.

✓ Call preparation.

✓ Quality of prepared questions.

✓ Quality of agenda.

✓ Objection handling.

✓ Listening.

✓ Quality of executing objectives in a call.

✓ Ideas on how to increase the size of a deal or customer relationship.

✓ Ideas on how to better negotiate.

✓ Ideas on how to improve the odds of closing business or closing business sooner.

...and much more, potentially, but keep the list manageable and simple. I recommend just three areas of focus at a time. You will probably want to change them up regularly, but keep the process simple.

Other ideas to consider include:

✓ Have a riding partner fill out a form critiquing the previous list after each call, and turn it in to a manager for review.

✓ Consider having a representative from the sales team create and name the coaching form.

✓ Require that the evaluator point out both observed strengths of each area and ideas for improvement.

✓ Coach participants on being constructive in their critiques and to always have specific ideas for improvement.

✓ Require all those receiving evaluations, ideas, or comments to *not* respond to suggestions, and those getting suggestions should go under a "ban of silence"—otherwise ideas will tend to dry up. When people feel that the partner will always have an excuse, they will be less likely to offer any insights. Thus you may have to have an evaluation area asking how well and "silently" those on the receiving end of the ideas responded.

✓ Tie one or more of the team calling objectives to overall organizational or sales team objectives (for example, increasing margins, sales call productivity, closing ratios, and so on).

✓ Alternate reps evaluating each other on team sales calls.

✓ Make team phone calls. Team calls don't only need to be face-to-face calling efforts; phone contacts can be a highly effective area to team in (and at much lower cost).

✓ Don't limit team calls to sales producers riding with each other; consider this an opportunity to have different facets of management engage not only with sales but customers as well. Also consider occasionally including team members from product management, engineering, service, or support.

✓ Get all hands on deck to address productivity that is lower than the potential or to quickly penetrate a territory that is new or has been somewhat ignored. It can be quite effective to put as many people into this target territory as possible to make joint sales calls and see the maximum number of prospects and customers. The teaming tends to ensure that everyone is productive and making as many calls as possible. The result is proof that a much greater number of calls can be made. Also, it can be a bit of a shock for the market and prospects to experience your company coming out in full force, making quite a powerful impression.

Going up the Ladder With the Sales Team Calling Strategy

King Calls. Involving presidents, GMs, and owners on calls can miraculously improve credibility, shortening sales cycles, and improving the sales efforts. Customers and reps appreciate the respect that is shown by occasionally having the top echelon out in the field. Many of the best CEOs, even in the Fortune 500, make this a regular practice. We have seen clients significantly increase the closing ratios on the largest 1 to 5 percent deals when the King Call strategy is used and the C-level is actively engaging with major accounts. The King Call strategy has singlehandedly brought incremental seven figures of income to eight- and nine-figure companies and divisions. Your "King" or "Queen" may be one of your best sales weapons currently sitting on the bench.

Sales Shouldn't Be a Lonely War

Selling is one of the most emotionally draining roles in your business. One's self esteem is put to the test with each challenge, objection, and rejection. Unlike most competition—such as sports, or even war—sales is usually a fight that one person is making on his or her own. Worse yet, if you fail in a sales call or series of efforts, you not only face the initial rejection but also the cross-examination and second-guessing from management and peers. But with team calls spaced appropriately you'll catch slumps and problems before they get out of hand. Implementing an effective team calling strategy will help your team sharpen their effectiveness, maintain a higher morale, and ultimately increase sales and profits. Determine where you could make team sales calls and then watch sales improve.

Get Sales Managers to Better Serve Their Primary Customer

Most sales managers I ask say that the single most important task they must improve in order to increase sales is spending more quality time with each rep. Yet this is the task that often gets the least amount of attention. Here is how to get sales managers focused on what matters most: their primary customer, the sales team.

Peel Back Their Role and Responsibilities and Reset the Priorities

Have your sales managers been loaded up with activities that aren't mission-critical, or that could be eliminated or delegated to lower cost employees? If most of your sales managers came up through sales, then they are likely to have the typical weaknesses sales producers have: They might not be as effective in managing and following up on details as they are with managing people, and yet many companies let this position devolve into an administrative role.

Here are some steps to redirect sales management's focus on the highest priorities:

✓ Conduct an innovation process around what can be eliminated from sales management's role.

✓ Prioritize sales management's list of duties.

✓ Determine what the time allotments for each priority should ideally be, given the reduced level of constraints.

✓ Consider conducting a "time study" of sales managers' time. We use a device they can carry with them, into which they can indicate, with the push of one button, what type of activity they are beginning to work on. After our two-week study, most are shocked to see the results—how little time goes to the highest priorities and how much time goes to the lowest priorities. I'm more concerned about managing sales managers' time than that of sale producers!

✓ Set objectives. Encourage a minimum amount of phone time and travel time with each rep (ideally you should have the sales managers set their own objectives on these targets).

✓ Measure the results of field and phone time reps are receiving, through basic calendar appointments and/or evaluation and coaching forms.

✓ Share results and best practices in sales manager "Echelons & Echeloning Sessions" (discussed in the next section).

Accelerate Sales Innovations With Echeloning Sessions

Too many sales reps and teams are islands, only managed by numbers and activity. Simply put, echelons are groups of six to eight individuals assembled to regularly exchange growth ideas in what I call Echeloning Sessions. These sessions usually take no longer than an hour, are held on a monthly to quarterly basis, and serve the purpose of giving a forum for sales producers to share growth ideas in an expeditious manner. The echeloning process can and probably should be facilitated in many other areas of your company. For our purpose here I'll detail how to facilitate them with your sales team.

Creating sales echelons and starting regular Echeloning Sessions for your sales and perhaps even other teams will aid your sales process by accelerating the sharing of best practices and innovation. Echeloning helps to unite sales teams, especially those spread across the country or around the world working remotely. Echeloning also develops confidence with new sales producers, as everyone is required to contribute their own ideas and suggestions to others. Less experienced sales reps hear how the most experienced have faced similar challenges, and every step of the sessions is focused on positive ideas or solutions to challenges.

The first step is forming the echelons. In some cases it may be best to keep the same team together throughout the year. In most cases I recommend that you consider rotating the roster of each echelon group so that each member gets exposed to more of the rest of their teammates.

Before starting the sales echeloning process I have usually interviewed many from the sales team and asked what their top challenges are and what they would like to improve regarding internal communication and information exchange. Invariably, the vast majority of sales producers within our clients are crying out for such a forum.

Echelon Meeting Guidelines and Flow

I recommend creating a form that each participant can fill out. That way, your team will come better prepared, and the notes can be shared much more efficiently if these forms are collected, compiled, and distributed.

The meeting includes input from each rep around what we call "The good, the bad, and the new."

- ✓ **The Good.** Have you ever noticed how easy it is for sales producers to brag about their successes? People like to share good news, and this is an easy way to get people to open up. Most everyone will have a success story to share on a monthly basis. The objective of sharing these success stories is to uncover the reasons for success so that the others on the team will learn from it. As the facilitator you will need to make an effort to tie every success story back to a best practice or lesson. You will direct your team to bring a story of a success, an implementation, or a change they have made that perhaps the others could benefit from knowing about. Even if it is not directly beneficial to the others in the group, the creativity and unique aspects behind it may inspire a similar change among team members. Don't fret about whether it's a major issue; it can be a very minor change or twist to the sales producer's personal daily routines, or something much broader, affecting the company as a whole.

- ✓ **The Bad.** You will ask everyone to also bring a personal challenge on which others can brainstorm. Everyone is always facing some challenge or problem—personally, departmentally, or organizationally—that could be thrown on the table for a "mind dump." You want them to bring up an issue that could benefit from getting different points of view. The problem you must prevent in this area of the session is that of people turning it into a bitch session about the company or home office. If this might be an issue with your team, firmly establish the guideline that these challenges must be areas around which sales producers have personal control and influence, and not issues about the company that are outside the sales team's control. The purpose of the meeting is to share ideas for growth, not complain.

✓ **The New.** At the echeloning meetings each member must bring a new idea or innovation that the others might be able to implement.

Echelon meetings should flow this way: One person should time the meeting to keep it on track and ensure that one member's issues don't excessively run over. Each member, or reporter, reads through or expounds on his or her Good story, New ideas, and Bad issue/problem/opportunity to get feedback.

After each reporter finishes his or her three points, he or she may be asked brief questions, but as soon as any team member begins to give feedback, especially on the Bad/Challenge issue, the one reporting goes under a **ban of silence**—this is imperative. There should be no spoken responses or comments on any feedback. The one reporting shouldn't even have any negative facial reactions; he or she should only be attentively listening or giving nods to indicate he or she is hearing the points. This magical guideline eliminates politics, arguments, and, most importantly, the reluctance to brainstorm feedback. This may be a powerful tactic to apply in your other meetings to ensure 100 percent feedback and participation while eliminating conflict and run-on meetings. In addition, innovation research proves clearly that it's not the quality of ideas that a group generates but the quantity and variety of ideas—and premature debate is the death knell of ideas and innovation.

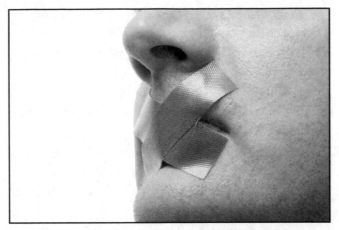

Instituting a "Ban of Silence" on meeting participants who are receiving feedback helps the flow of ideas and shortens meetings.

Depending on the number of attendees, you will need to have a predetermined target time allotted for each report, and someone to keep an eye on the clock. The best echeloning meetings usually take between 45 and 90 minutes.

Some companies actually have echelons of sales teams gather for half days and full days every month to go through a similar format. In these types of environments they are usually covering much more information, like reporting out of the total number of phone dials, sales calls, active prospects, deals and dollar amounts closed, and the like. I have seen sales teams become absolutely addicted to even the full-day version of these meetings. They see them as the most important accountability, training, and goal-setting opportunity of their month or quarter.

Here is a sample note that could be sent to the team announcing the kickoff of sales Echeloning Sessions:

Team,

I'm writing to review the outline and purpose
of the Echeloning meeting so that we are getting
these off on the right foot. here is what you want to
remember and come prepared for:

Echeloning meetings are about one thing: the
sales team exchanging **ideas that will help all of you
to MAKE MORE MONEY.**

The outline is simple and the time invested
is short; a maximum of one hour per month or
less, based on our following the timeline and the
frequency of the meetings.

Everyone must come prepared to share three
things:

1. A **success story** that others might learn
    an idea or principle from. Every month all
    of you have successes that we could learn
    from, so pick one, share it in just a couple of
    minutes, and tell us what you think the lesson
    or moral of the story is.

2. A **new idea** that other sales reps could
    implement. This could be an idea you use,
    or even something totally new that you
    read about in a book or heard through the
    grapevine. ANY idea that just might help you
    or others sell more and make more money.

3. A **personal challenge** or personal
    improvement area. EVERYONE can improve
    on something, so pick one area, issue,
    or challenge you have with how you work,
    a customer, or **something over which you**

as the sales rep can influence or control,
and share it so that others can brainstorm
ideas for improvement. Even if you are the
best salesperson on the team, this process
helps everyone build ideas that can grow their
business. Don't let pride or fear prevent you
from sharing an improvement area; this is
often the most valuable part of the meeting,
and the team is committing to each other to
help everyone grow. We can't be islands.

BAN OF SILENCE: After each person has
presented the above three areas, they go under a ban
of silence. As people share ideas there must be no
comment, as any feedback can cause the drying-up of
new ideas.

EVERY person is required to speak for at least 10
seconds on any idea they can come up with on how
the presenter might be able to solve their problem or
improve the situation. Just brainstorm; there are no
bad ideas.

The timer of the meeting will move things along
and may cut you off if a comment runs too long so
as to ensure the Echeloning part of the meeting never
runs over an hour. Don't take it personally.

Thanks in advance for your preparation and
sharing of ideas.

Implementing Echeloning Sessions

Think about who would be the best candidates for you to invite to the first Echeloning Sessions, and facilitate a few meetings,
knowing that you will learn of some details you'll want to roll into

future meetings. Also consider other areas in your company where the same type of format would help in exchanging best practices and innovations in a much more rapid manner than is happening currently. You will be impressed at the wealth of information that lies untapped within your team, and how fast you can team-build while accelerating growth.

Ensure You Have the Right People on Your Sales Team

A mistake that often demoralizes a team is management's unrealistic expectations about personality types and skill sets within sales team members. When you are recruiting candidates for an accounting or marketing position, the skills, character, and psychological attributes you are looking for are usually congruent—for example, "detailed-oriented numbers crunchers" or "creatively minded writers." Yet too often companies attempt to recruit, train, and motivate sales professionals toward an unrealistic combination of skills and attributes, such as a "self-motivated and independent individual" who is also compliant with onerous policies, or the "creative and influential communicator who is also detail-oriented and money-motivated," yet complacent with slow-paying incentives and bonus plans.

Many sales professionals have a few key talents that have the potential to be the foundation of success. It is just a matter of focusing on what strengths they might have, and, by working together with them, diminishing the impact of their weaknesses. This is the classic definition of management—leveraging strengths and minimizing the impact of weaknesses. The following are a few key strategies to leveraging the unique talents of a diverse sales force.

You should use profiling instruments in the hiring process, and it can be most valuable to start by profiling your most successful sales producers. On larger teams you will usually be able to identify common traits among your top performers. The traits may vary from one company to the next due to culture, and from one industry to the next. But if you can uncover the common DNA within your top performers, your ability to hire, motivate, and align the team will be much easier.

My company offers profiling instruments, but I'm wary of clients over-relying on them. Nothing can surpass the value of an excellent interviewing process that is based on a quality outline of questions and thorough reference and cross-reference checking. Detailing the interviewing process is not the purpose of this book; however, it is potentially critical in a turnaround or growth effort, so you can contact our office for more information on how to conduct excellent evaluation interviews and onboarding processes.

Chapter 11
Stop Selling Products and Start Selling Profit

Creating a Culture Focused on Customer Profit Builds Your Profits

Profit is often maligned as a bad thing in our culture as large companies are chastised for monopolistic actions and "grossly excessive profits," as some would call them. Because of this environment, many of your employees may be tainted with an improper appreciation for the requirement of profit as a way to deliver and measure value for customers. It is your job as a leader to create the right context for the profit focus—both for your company and the profits you help to deliver for others, especially your customer.

I'm shocked by the number of struggling companies where there is widespread misconception that the company is "doing quite well," and the belief is that "the owners make some huge profits...they are just swimming in it!" Open-book management—in other words, showing the meaning behind the fiscal numbers and many of your company's actual numbers—has a transforming impact on employees. Obviously specific individuals' compensation is not revealed, but the total cost of compensation along with everything else is usually a shock to most employees. You'll have to debate whether to show the profits or not, but if there are few or none to show, then it can become a transformative exercise. People begin to realize that their jobs are at stake and everyone needs to be a part of the profit improvement process or ultimately there will be no company, no jobs.

Many employees struggle with the process of uncovering how much your solutions can improve a customer's position and profits, thinking, "Our solution and benefits are just so obvious!" What most employees lack are an adequate questioning vocabulary and a focus on the customer's appreciation of profit. Most employees think the business that your company is in has to do with the product or the service, but not the result that the customer is buying. This is an inadequate understanding of what a customer values and can be a potential root of a business's demise.

Facilitating a shift in focus that is not just on the customer but also on what the customer values and thus the profit you deliver can be a key to your accelerated growth or a turnaround.

Presidential Commitment to a Value-Focused Philosophy

The philosophical direction of a team is set by you as its titular leader. Whether you are the president or a manager of a small unit, you have the responsibility to direct where your team members put their focus and what is valued as a team. One such focus you must foster in your team is that of working to improve the profits of your customers.

Presidents put the imprimatur on the mission statement, so if it is lacking in any aspect, the responsibility lays at their feet. Therefore, a powerful aspect that presidents can include in the mission is a statement that declares the priority of improving the profitability of the customers. It may seem like a minor issue or lip service, but missions can impact the actions of employees and impressions with customers. If you have the chutzpah to add a phrase emphasizing the importance your company puts on improving the profitability of your customers, I believe it will accelerate your growth.

There are some businesses in which *profitability* isn't the best word, and perhaps *value* or some other equivalent is, but in most business-to-business environments, *profitability* is the perfect word to emphasize your focus on the customer. "Improving our customers' profits" is a phrase that will capture their attention, and as you use other tools to prove your impact, you will increase customer retention as well.

President

The focus on "Customers' Profit" begins at the top.

Profitability Values and Objectives

A focus on improving profitability for the customer can also be represented in your values. Values become a guiding force with your team and they are empowered by including clear, customer-focused values to make more significant decisions that will mutually benefit the customer and you. A focus on increasing the customer's profitability may become a competitive advantage if you are able to make it an obvious and pervasive focus in your people and processes.

You should set specific marketing objectives that revolve around improving your customers' profits through improved service and innovations. If your team can discover effective methods to measure, research, improve, and prove how you are increasing your customers' profitability, then you will have a powerful marketing and sales tool. Letting your customers know of this type of objective and engaging them in the process of achieving it will lock them in. Few companies take marketing, innovation, and a focus on what the customers value to such depth.

Foster Innovation in Proposals and Pricing With Options

A significant amount of growth potential for your company may lie in how you position, package, and price your proposals. Much potential in customer relationships is lost by not positioning the relationship in proposals from the outset as a partnership, a relationship based on continuous improvement and improved profit. Get your team to change the way they look at an agreement with a customer: that it is not just a proposed transaction but a "Partnering Plan" that has built-in measures of success that can and will be reviewed to help secure agreement of successful completion as well as commitment to future work.

Regardless of your success with proposals, you would do well to go through a proposal innovation effort. The vast majority of companies could make great strides in this area. Your proposals should not be the tool that does the selling but a summation of what has been conceptually agreed upon in previous conversations with an economic buyer. The What, Why, Who, When, and How are summarized to reaffirm in the buyer's mind why this project is so valuable and why your proposed steps (and you as the prospective partner) are a great choice. That said, proposals give you a chance to help facilitate upselling with options that might be more profitable than what your team is proposing and/ or larger than what the customer originally requested. The question is, with some innovations and quality enhancements, could your proposal process improve your positioning, profits, and closing ratios? In most cases, the answer is yes.

An excellent outline to follow is what we call a Partnering Plan. This is an agreement that includes not only what needs to be done, but also what the impact and value of that relationship will foster, as well as other options that might actually expand the relationship, out of the gate. Repositioning your relationship with customers as a partnership and a process as opposed to a transaction and event helps to put the focus on what they value most and the incremental profit you can deliver, instead of putting the focus and negotiation on price.

Even if your business doesn't use proposals, consider using the following concepts of objectives, measures, and value.

✓ Partnering Plan—A F.O.C.U.S.ed Proposal Outline

    ✗ **Facts & Situation Overview:** A restatement of the issues involved.

    ✗ **Objectives/Outcomes:** The customer's desired outcomes.

    ✗ **Counts/Measures/Metrics:** The indicators for determining progress and success. What will be counted to measure progress?

    ✗ **Upside Value:** The dollarized impact and benefits of successful completion of the project.

    ✗ **Solution Steps & Methodology:** An outline of the steps required.

✓ Timing: Start, duration, and ending dates.

✓ Joint Accountabilities: What the customer and you commit to do together.

- ✓ Credentials/Differentiators: A brief citation of why you are the best source, and references if appropriate.

- ✓ Options: A choice of options to meet the objectives. They will very both in the value they deliver to the customer and in your pricing.

- ✓ Terms and Conditions: Fees and payment terms for each option.

Although there are many similar proposal outlines, a unique aspect of the one just listed is in the "partnering" and the process of follow-up and accountability for results. These are aspects that increase closure rates and tighten the relationship. The process also allows for a mutual confirmation of the value your company has delivered, and thus increases the likelihood of customer retention.

Three of the most important facets of this proposal outline are the customer objectives, measures, and value. When your team is selling effectively, they aren't just trading your products or services; rather, they are consulting and/or partnering with the customer to improve their position, the customer's profits. If your team hasn't identified clear objectives from your buyer relative to what you are selling, they haven't even begun to sell; rather, they are peddling or presenting, hoping to hit a nerve of interest—they are shooting in the dark. Identifying objectives can be as simple as asking, "In relation to this area, what are your top objectives?" or, "What are the top problems you'd most like to do away with or at least improve upon?"

Your team's ability to clarify customer objectives is only a fraction of what is required to properly position your solution so that the customer's focus will be on your value and not your price. Your team must clarify the full impact, especially financially, and ideally in the terms of the customer's own words and not your own estimates. This can become a trigger for accelerating your sales cycles and your customers' buy-in. Asking, "What would the benefits be of solving that problem or reaching that objective?"

will get you close, but you will need to press further and identify what they might expect the dollarized value of each benefit to be. Having this conversation is the heart of being a true sales consultant—in other words, a partner with your customers in reaching their objectives.

"Measures" are the metrics that determine whether you've done your job and fulfilled your promise to deliver progress toward their objective. They answer the statement, "We know we will have been successful in this effort if..." Agreeing on measures is yet another factor in differentiating you from the competition that is ready to sell and run. You are setting up the relationship for the next sale by putting in place milestones and touch points where your team and the customer will confirm that the results are being delivered. The benefit of setting up this process is that it will not only tee you up for the next sale with this customer, but it will also increase your odds of gathering more testimonials and referrals that will help you in marketing and selling more business.

Like good leaders, the better negotiators and sales professionals detail the next several steps of a relationship—the timing, specific actions, and future points of discussion and review. These points are included in the outline under Objectives/Outcomes, Counts/Measures/Metrics, Upside Value, Solution Steps/Methodology, Timing, and Accountability. The document calls the two parties back to it for a regular review. It helps to lock in customers—and in a turnaround situation, you need to be as locked in to them as you can be.

Well-prepared proposals not only open up the opportunity for future growth but also allow for expansion of the sale at the start of the relationship.

Pool Tables and Girl Scout Cookies

There is an old story about a chain of stores that sold pool tables. A few locations were greatly outselling all of the others.

Upon investigation, the management discovered that the most successful locations had innovated beyond the rules! Secret shoppers were readying to write up the stores for several infractions. First, these rule-breakers had the most expensive pool tables on display at the front of the store, where the sun and children were likely to do damage. The sales personnel were also ignoring the directive to get the customer's price range of interest and start selling to that range. Instead, the sales process included a full walk-through of all the different pricing options, starting with the most expensive pool tables first. The philosophy and benefits of these unique, high-end pieces were fully explained: "Lifetime guarantee/relationship," "custom hand-crafted pieces of art," and other points of value. Once these unique benefits were understood by the customer, this caused them to spend many more times what the average customer spent at the stores that sold by the rules.

The point is, customers can't spend more with you if they aren't aware of the value offered through your highest-priced and best options.

In another story, the Girl Scout who was not only selling a great deal of cookies but was selling more and more each year was invited to share her strategies. She explained several of her innovations that included good territory management and mapping of her ideal "markets/neighborhoods." But the keys to her success lay in her proposing of options, from the most expensive to the least. She also had tickets to a fundraiser ball to sell, and she was the number-one seller on that front as well. She said, "The good thing was that they were expensive—a lot more expensive than the cookies. But they were worth every penny. Between the chefs from the best restaurants that created a world-class five-course meal to the great entertainment, it made for a date night like no other, it was a great deal. And although each ticket was over a hundred dollars, there was a huge discount if you bought two pairs for a double-date night."

After that sell, by the time she got to the cookie conversation many people were relieved. She asked how many people were in the household and captured their names on her "proposal." With her prospect holding a picture of all the products/cookies in hand she would then mention each family member's name and ask what cookies they most enjoyed. She'd make a note next to their name as to their favorites. Then she asked if the family had a freezer. Once her prospect was thoroughly profiled and qualified, she was able to propose her options: "As you mentioned, your family really likes the treat of having our special cookies. But as you know, we only come around once a year, and the only thing worse than anyone not having their own boxes of their favorites is having those boxes run out in just a few months after you've ordered them. Since our cookies are made to be just as tasty after being frozen, my happiest customers stock up for a full year. Or there are several other options. Here is how many of the boxes you would need to keep your entire family happy for the entire year— I call that the gold option. Second, here is how many boxes you would need to keep your family happy for just half the year, the silver option. Finally here is how many boxes you would need to keep your family happy for three months. But you tell me, what do you think everyone in your family would like you to choose, the gold, silver, or bronze option?"

Now, I'm not a big fan of hard closes, but I do like the fact that this girl cared enough to do the work for the customer and figure out what the three possible options might be. And based on her high "renewal rate" with customers, many obviously liked the options.

Most options you will have in your business aren't as simple as cookies and pool tables, but the principle of giving options to allow you to raise the bar of potential with many deals will capture you incremental new business, and showing a third option that might be below the scope of what was asked for but is still clearly profitable for you, can help to save many deals that you might otherwise lose.

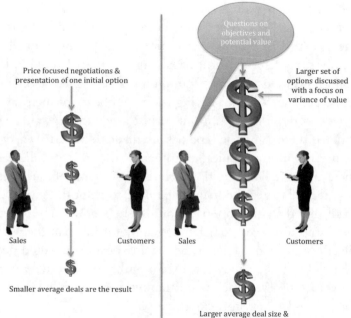

Effectively implementing tools to increase average deal size can be the game-changer for companies in turnaround mode, and can give an immediate boost to most any company.

Use Well-Structured Options to Reduce Price Haggling and Protect Profits

Because many are vexed by questions like, "What should we charge?" "What is their investment threshold?" and, "Did we leave too much on the table?" an effective way to overcome those concerns, reduce haggling and unnecessary negotiations, and close more deals is to offer a set of options rather than just a yes/no decision. Buyers can negotiate with themselves as to how deeply they want to engage your services or invest in your products by choosing just one, all, or a combination of your options.

Give your team the tools to offer flexibility in options without implying to customers that there is flexibility in price. Negotiate value/options, rather than negotiating away your profits by cutting your price. If your team is concerned about going over your customers' budget, show them how they can reduce the amount of services/product/value you will deliver, keep price integrity, and yet still secure a profitable engagement.

Using Partnering Plans to Secure the Next Purchase

At a summation of an engagement, you can use the Partnering Plan to show how you've fulfilled the promise, and fill the buyer in on other details such as the value of your successful interventions. As mentioned in Chapter 8, this is where the testimonial letter tactic can be used to show the full array of benefits and value delivered. The points under the objectives, measures, and value sections from your original Partnering Plan often make up the outline of the post-engagement summary letter. Now your team has an instant letter of reference that can lead to still more business from that client and help you secure more business with new prospects.

Good proposal outlines with the aforementioned required fields of information filled in also beget a healthier selling approach in which the team is reminded to get the "right stuff" that will close more deals. Compare the Partnering Plan outline to your current proposals and make sure your team is selling on all cylinders.

Imagine, if your company is in a struggle for survival, and your sales team has a current closing ratio of 25 percent, with ideas like these you can increase it to 35 percent. Now imagine that with the tactic of asking for more by offering bigger options, you are able to increase the average size of orders by 25 percent. The synergy of these two leverage points may very well enable you to increase sales by 50 to 80 percent, and increase profit margins by a few significant points as well.

Use the F.O.C.U.S. Questioning Vocabulary

The reason many companies get into trouble is that sales has stopped asking for the customer's take on the value the supplier can or does deliver. This can happen in your company when sales fails to ask the right questions that will uncover the amount of impact your solutions can or do have.

Here is how to create a custom questioning vocabulary for your team. This process will improve your team's focus on your customers, thereby improving their profits, and thus resulting in fewer price negotiations and a differentiation of your business in the marketplace.

Several top problems are evident when the sales process and questioning effectiveness lack the proper focus and approach:

✓ Qualification of prospects is nonexistent, infrequent, or ineffective.

✓ Negotiations about price are frequent.

✓ Juxtapositioning of your proposals against competition are common.

✓ Delays in decision-making are common, thus elongating sales cycles and the costs of each sales call.

✓ Even after winning business, customers may question or not fully appreciate the value and impact that your service provides.

Since 1990, we have ridden with hundreds of the top-performing sales professionals in the country. We've seen that this approach to sales improvement can frequently be at the heart of transforming the sales organization overall. It is not the teaching of this questioning strategy that is important so much as facilitating a team in creating their own custom questions focused on the unique positioning their firm has in the industry.

The vast majority of excellent sales professionals aren't excellent because they are backslapping, relationship-focused rapport builders, but rather because they are value-focused, and work to divine the potential of a relationship and a customer's future with adroitly focused questions. They discover untapped profit potentials in a Socratic process with the help of the customer. And because people tend to support that which they help to create, the excellent sales professionals leave their customers feeling more a part of a partnership than on the receiving end of a pitch or a push–pull style of selling.

The top-echelon sales professionals and average sales professionals who've risen to the level of true profit-discovery consultants we've studied have done so because they've mastered the art of questioning and focus on customers' potential new profits. You could call this approach Selling by Objectives, or SBO.

To sell by the customer's objectives and help them to discover new profits, the hard style of closing so often taught and mis-applied is far surpassed by true consulting and profit discovery. Rather than closing, sales professionals who are true consultants *advance the sale* and are more often giving their prospects a choice of options rather than the yes/no stress of a hard close.

Getting to that point of empowering a team to be true con-sultants takes the effort of customizing questions that clarify the profits being lost to inaction and profits to be gained with the implementation of the best solution. There are five types of ques-tions that can be asked in the selling process. We call this the F.O.C.U.S. Questioning Method.

1. **Fact questions** elicit data that is of a neutral importance to the customer. Although some fact questions may be critical to qualifying or appropriately presenting the right solutions to your customer, poor sales performers get caught up in asking *too many* fact questions—many of which may be of little importance and/or could be found through basic preparation before or after the initial call.

2. **Opportunity questions** elicit customers' objectives, problems, pains, or direction toward which they need to move. Most often the answers tweak a pain; it could be the pain of an unsolved problem or the pain of not moving as fast as possible toward a valid objective or result.

3. **Consequence questions** (can also be called **cost questions**) elicit the cost of *not* solving that problem or reaching that objective. Cost questions quantify the negative dollarization of the problem or inaction. Sometimes the consequences are merely emotional, but in most business situations an excellent questioner/consultant/sales professional can help a customer

discover the dollarized costs of the opportunities discovered.

4. **Upside questions** help to understand the value that stands to be gained if a change is made, the problem is solved, or the objective is reached sooner with an intervention that has yet to be decided upon.

5. **Solution Step questions** clarify the next steps that help to advance the sale/relationship and often give the customer a choice of options rather than a yes/no close. Most complex sales aren't closed as much as they are advanced to the next step if proper qualification has taken place at each step.

There are several key competencies needed to get a team to become proficient in questioning like consultants rather than pushy peddlers:

✓ They need to understand the different types of questions as well as the value of the information they gain.

✓ They need to understand the unique positioning your firm has in the industry.

✓ They should be a part of the process in creating the questioning vocabulary.

✓ The list of questions should be ever evolving, improving, and tweaked as new ideas and questions are refined.

✓ The F.O.C.U.S.ed questioning process should lead into your proposal formulation. Each of the F.O.C.U.S. question types correlates to respective proposal sections. For example, the answers to the objective questions will be inserted into the Objectives section of the proposal, and so on.

✓ Ongoing coaching from teammates and/or managers should be de rigueur in the process of continuous improvement of the sales process and marketing efforts.

A quality outline in your proposal template not only reinforces the F.O.C.U.S. concept but also puts the focus on customers' desired outcomes. Ensure your proposal outline compels the sales professional to get the right information to truly build a business case that is the work of good consulting and discovery.

An ROI Analysis With Customers Can Improve Customer Retention

If your customer relationships aren't reaching their full potential, it may be because your customer doesn't see the value of more fully engaging with you. In this case, a powerful marketing tool is to conduct an ROI analysis as to what the specific return might be to your customers if they were to more fully engage or purchase a solution from you.

Consider having your team survey individual influencers throughout the prospective company as to the severity of the problems you can solve and the value of doing so. Your team will need to think of how to best position such an effort. I have had clients who were able to just position this approach with something as simple as a "No-Cost Profit Improvement Assessment."

You may have a situation in which surveying your prospect's customers (or customers' customers) is where you will find the greatest profit improvement areas for your customer. Using the approach described in Chapter 6, consider becoming your customers' third party for uncovering the untapped potentials with their customers or prospects.

Often the work and time involved in such a marketing and selling effort will be less than a typical sales cycle. Plus, you will have the added benefit of triangulating or confirming the potential profit improvement you will be able to bring your customer.

Top Leaders Set the Focus and Drive the Agenda

The bottom line is, the tools in this chapter will help to shift the focus in your company from products to profits, both for your company and your customers'. When this happens you will be inoculated from the sickness of commodity-focused selling and purchasing, and your margins will be protected and expand to their appropriate level. But it is the titular leader and top management team that must work in tandem to facilitate this shift in focus and encourage or lead these projects to ensure that your profits aren't just protected but also growing during your turnaround.

Chapter 12
Aiming for Growth With Your Sales Team

The Stretch Target Concept

What would happen to your revenues if you could increase the size of your average customer by 50 percent? What would happen to your profitability if you could fire your bottom 10 percent of customers and replace them with the same number of customers that are the size of your current top 1 percent—or even much larger? What would the impact be if just 10 percent of your mid- to top-level sales producers doubled their production because half of their new customers were now two, three, or even five times the average customer? I have seen these very results occur with the strategies outlined here.

Sales producers (and companies in general) often get caught in ruts of thinking as to what is possible and what their growth rate or average customer size should be. You as part of management must coach your team to focus on the company's greatest results and relationships—and how much more they could be in the future. Then you should show them how they can replicate and multiply those same efforts and results in the future to realize much larger relationships.

You can use this concept to facilitate a quantum leap by showing a team how they can bring on new customers that are many times larger than their current largest customers. Here are the steps.

Create Top Customer Lists

Create lists for the company's top 1 percent and top 20 percent customers. Do the same for each individual sales producer, selling team, or division.

Just as I wrote in Chapter 7 (on growth-oriented targeting), it is critical that you ensure that every division and every sales producer is always aware of who their top customers are, based on total net profits. Your team needs to have these prioritized lists printed and in front of their eyes for regular review for several reasons:

1. They will give these priority customers more attention and thus will improve retention.

2. They will be better able to profile and qualify who your best types of customers are.

3. They will do a better job of investing more time going after more of these better customers—and less time with time-sucking low-profit customers. Quick-tip: Recommend your profit-draining customers to the competition!

Create Top Prospect Lists

Have every sales producer list out "whale targets," or what I call "stretch target lists," of prospects that are two, three, or even five times larger than their largest current clients. There will need to be some balance as far as what is realistic, but you need to challenge the status quo and false paradigms of customer size potential. Usually in our employee interviews during our customary preparation for engagements, our consultants will have spoken with many of the top customers, salespeople, and managers, and we will have uncovered insights as to what is possible regarding the largest potential relationships on which our client could realistically focus. Usually a few of the top sales producers are significantly outside the norm and have a larger-than-average customer profile. These top-echelon sales producers have much of the information that you need to help win this higher-margin, larger-than-average-value customer. You must become the expert in asking for, listening to, and facilitating these golden insights throughout the company.

The question then becomes, What is the appropriate time balance between the mid-sized bread-and-butter prospects that may or may not have a higher closing ratio, and much larger potential customers? The ratios might be lower with larger customers, but even so, with much larger volume and perhaps margin, the ROI for the time invested could be much higher. I am shocked at how many businesses have equal or even higher closing ratios with larger customers, but for a variety of reasons, sales and marketing have focused on smaller accounts. The bottom-line is, you must regularly discern the right balance and push the envelope toward growing average client size and deal size to its optimal level by getting every sales producer to consistently put the right amount of effort toward a much larger customer size and percent of customer share.

Ask, Don't Tell to Get More Growth (Socratic Stretch)

As I discuss throughout the book, it is best to get your sales producers and others involved to define what they think is possible after you have presented as much evidence as you can that the bar can be raised. Because people tend to support that which they help to create, you will get more buy-in by getting your team to set the targets rather than you telling them what you think they should be. Socratically sell your team; don't tell your team the potential.

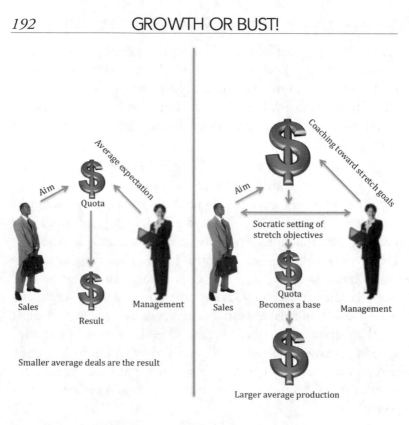

Effectively implementing tools to increase average sales producer performance can potentially bring significant leaps in growth.

Socratically set goals around increasing the following:

✓ **Number of new "stretch target customers."** You must make sure your team targets enough larger stretch customers, and also that these targets are as large as the sales producers believe they can possibly be. Each of your sales producers could have varying numbers of stretch target prospects; the right number of stretch targets might be as few as one or as many as 40 or hundreds. Your task is to get this number up to the maximum; if you don't, what may happen is that with too few targets, your sales producers may experience failures or roadblocks with the stretch targets listed due to the quantity of the list, not the quality.

✓ **Average share of existing customers.** You can facilitate a separate stretch effort for the purpose of expanding the share of your current customers. Many companies with a "maintainer" mentality and culture will have a preponderance of sales producers who are only getting a small percentage of the potential from their average customer. You can have an outside third party survey your customers to see what percentage of business is going to other companies, and you can have your sales team ask the question as well, but you must find out what the potential averages are in your market. You may also have a few top sales producers who are clearly proving that a much higher percentage of customer share is a reality. Once you discern the realities, you need to determine just how far that average can be pushed throughout your team and get the team to aim for the maximum. This is an excellent area to facilitate an innovation process and a regular sharing of best practices. Let those succeeding share what is working and keep testing for what methods can most easily be scaled throughout the team, especially with your less experienced sales producers.

✓ **Average share of new customers.** The same type of effort you are doing with existing customers can be done with prospects or new customers. Get your team to also stretch how much they ask for from the new customer in proposals and closing options (I discussed more on this in Chapter 11). In many businesses the percentage share you have of the customer's total spend for your offerings (a.k.a. share of customer) is also a stretch potential. I have seen so many sales producers and managers become content with having a small percentage of each customer's potential spend—say, 10 or 20 percent. Yet after we conducted depth interviews with these customers we would find that many of them were spending 80 or 90 percent with a single competitor of our client. The competitor wasn't necessarily providing better returns to the customer but was asking for more of their business.

Get Sales Producers to Think in Terms of Quantum Leaps

The same principle of stretch targets can be applied to production throughout the course of a year. You should conduct an analysis with your sales producers regarding how long it took for them to multiply their sales production and/or incomes by a factor of two, three, or even five. Fivefold increases may seem like too much of a leap to you at first, but when you talk with commissioned sales producers, many can recall a time when they were earning one fifth of what they are currently earning. In industries where there is no cap on commission, and high six-figure incomes are common and seven-figure incomes are not unheard of, it is possible for sales producers to go back and see fivefold increases in their incomes more than once.

You need to pick the multiplier that makes sense for your environment and begin a conversation with sales producers about the time it took to increase by that percent. For example, you may show an instance when a beginning rep produced $200,000 in sales and $50,000 in commission to him in his first year. Three years later he was at $400,000 in sales and more than $100,000 in commission. Two years after that he was at $800,000 in sales and $250,000 in commission. He had a fourfold increase in sales revenue in six years. Yet tracking this on an Excel spreadsheet wouldn't have him doubling sales from that $800,000 level until around year 13, and the same for his income. The fact is that for sales producers who are consistently aiming for the highest possible achievements with no psychological restrictions on income, their rate of increase can and often does look like a hockey stick pattern in the first phase of their career.

Here is the key question to ask each salesperson: How much sooner could you double your sales this time, versus how long it took to double sales last time? And what is your plan for doing so? The amount of increase may be different; it could be a 50 percent increase instead of 100 percent. Regardless, you have got to get sales producers to see the pattern of success they or others have had, and how they have in most cases accelerated their rate of growth—they are not growing incrementally but exponentially. They should begin to see how they have in the past and can in the future grow exponentially based on their increased wisdom and future innovations and synergies yet untapped. You should coach them toward the highest potential rate of growth possible.

Build Sales Stretch Plans That Aim for Quantum Leaps

I recommend that at least one quarter per year—if not every quarter—sales producers should build an individualized stretch plan. These plans should include the most optimistic targets they can envision hitting in three-year, one-year, and quarterly increments. These targets are not conservative "odds are I could hit these" type targets, but rather, "If all the stars align, it is possible that I could achieve these levels of production." Again, you must assure everyone that they have total safety if they don't hit the goals, but they need the chance to expand their thinking.

The reason that these stretch goals are so valuable isn't just that production may increase; more importantly, stretch targets accelerate the rate of innovation. Thinking about bigger achievements begets thoughts about improvements that must happen to achieve such change. The thoughts become much different from the thoughts that are borne of quotas, like "How soon can I stop working?"

Granted, there must be realism in the targets and plans—that is your job as the facilitator of the process to keep balance yet exhort toward the maximum potentials.

How do you get your team to agree to such high goals?

In our **Stretch 100** sales strategy and innovation programs (which I'll get to in a moment) we get the promise from management that the sales team is allowed to fail on their stretch goals, and that the stretch goals, if reached, will not become the new quota.

Prep your team with the research you have on the market and the facts you have from internal company information and show that much higher potentials are possible, even if you aren't aiming to be the best. But this begs the question, Can and should your team aim to be the best? The majority of times, significant growth doesn't require a team or individuals to aim to be number one, but only to aim to reach a much higher already proven potential, which makes all of these strategies all the more realistic and achievable.

Set Blue-Sky Objectives

Have you ever seen an objective in business or in your personal life accomplished long before you expected it to be accomplished? Have you noticed how many people tend to complete a tremendous amount of their deliverables before a deadline? What you are seeing is either our subconscious never stopping for a rest or our own volition working actively and more openly to achieve. The challenge you may be facing in managing a team of diverse talent, experience, and confidence is that you can't be sure whom on your team succeeds unintentionally, and who is truly achieving on their intent.

You have probably seen some of the scads of research that shows that when our minds create a vision or a target for accomplishment, both our conscious and subconscious minds go to work to figure out how to accomplish the task. I won't go into the details about why this works, but I will challenge you to ask yourself, How well do you manage your team's focus on visionary potential? You must put in place management processes that allow both ends of the intention spectrum to succeed.

One of the processes through which we facilitate management and sales teams is called the **Stretch 100**, a sales strategy and innovation process focused on getting individual sales producers to create far more aggressive plans for growth after hearing of the best practices from within their team and industry as well as the insights of top customers and management.

I am fascinated and gratified when I come back approximately 100 days later (part of the reasoning behind the name "Stretch 100") and hear of the progress each participant has made. I have been shocked to see how many participants have reached three-year objectives in just three months! Granted, this isn't possible in businesses with earnings caps, but in industries like finance and commercial real estate, commodities like chemicals, or B2B businesses like software and consulting, it is quite possible for sales producers to have quantum leaps in short order. The key is a clear strategy and aggressive amounts of innovation.

Again, I make every president and sales manager we work with promise me and the team directly that their new stretch goals will not become their new quota. You must remember, one of the reasons sales producers sandbag and just barely reach their quota is that most of those in management look at sales producers just as the outdated economists looked at labor—as an expendable resource whose productivity should be ratcheted up to the maximum potential with little concern for the psychology and spirit of the individual.

I make the leadership promise the sales producers that they are allowed to fail when it comes to the stretch goals they set. The fact is that many *do* fail, and they fail miserably. But most often, for even those who missed their targets in a big way still made significant improvements in how they did their work, and even more importantly they increased their expected production.

What Matters to the Top Leader

Has the top leader of your company consistently communicated all of the following?

- ✓ The priority of significant growth and how everyone can contribute to accelerating the company's progress toward aggressive growth goals.

- ✓ The power, influence, and importance of the sales team's efforts and input regarding bringing on larger and higher-quality customers, and how sales can contribute in other ways that will help to grow profits and revenues.

- ✓ That his door is always open for anyone who has important insights on how we could grow sales.

- ✓ That she is eager to become personally involved in helping to close large deals or speak to other C-level executives with prospective new business, in phone calls, meetings, or whatever she can reasonably contribute in the effort to grow sales.

- ✓ That sales is as critical a function of the company as any other part of the company.

Have you noticed how frequently the titular leaders of companies come from accounting, engineering, product development, or some other non-sales-related function within a company? As a result, these leaders tend to gravitate toward the areas with which they are most comfortable and familiar. When you see communication from the top with a sales team become infrequent, you will soon see a sales team begin to feel like the black sheep of the corporate family. Perhaps you've experienced even more antagonistic environments for sales, where they may be viewed as the overpaid lollygaggers who golf and goof off as much as they may or may not work. Or perhaps you've experienced situations in which sales is in what seems to be a perpetual battle with marketing, production, or some other facet of the company. Sales sees the other groups as not listening to what the customers are demanding, and the other stakeholders in the company see sales as the whiny complainers that are never happy with the deliverables or directives.

When the titular head of a business has little to say about sales growth objectives or sales in general, many will sense that sales is a lower priority and thus work and produce accordingly. To tap the fuller sales growth potential it is imperative that the top leader communicates the importance of sales growth and exhorts the team accordingly. Many a sales turnaround makes it or breaks it based on the involvement of a business's top leader and his or her focus on new sales growth and the sales team.

Here are some best practices of top-echelon executives who value and extol sales as part of an aggressive growth focus:

✓ Going on key account calls and priority selling opportunities.

✓ Being involved in recognizing and delivering incentives with the sales team.

✓ Listening to the sales team for input on how to improve issues with the company and within the selling process and sales support.

Parachuting in for the national sales convention once a year doesn't do it. A frequent best practice of presidents is calling every single salesperson in private, one-on-one calls to ask specific questions about how the president and the company can better serve the sales team so that they can accelerate the growth of the company.

Some of the best leaders I have worked with, including presidents, COOs, and CEOs of Fortune 500 companies, have a minimum number of meetings with top customers with a chief focus being retaining and growing the account. One founder/CEO of one of the fastest-growing Fortune 500 companies of all time made it a point to meet with every top-20-percent customer and every single employee and location at least once a year. Although it filled much of his calendar, he said that this time with his team—and especially sales producers—was some of his most important work, with the highest ROI.

When the Board Hires the Next CEO

When the board of directors evaluates candidates for CEO or president, a top concern of theirs should be the involvement the future leader plans to have with the sales team, customers, and prospects, as well as his or her sales savvy. A leader that sees selling as something that is beneath him isn't a leader at all, and will probably be an antagonist of the growth potentials.

Chapter 13
The Role of the Turnaround Leader

Many turnaround situations involve a leader who is exhibiting a behavior that creates a wall between the company and progress, frustrating any activities that might correct the company's path and bring about growth. Whether you are that leader or an investor, board member, or other conservator, you must realize that turnaround begins at the top.

A Look at the Leader: Five Impediments to Turnaround and Growth

1. Pride

Unhealthy levels of pride contribute to a leader's failure to give credit to others when appropriate, or to an unwillingness to listen to customers, employees, and others, when their input would help the business. Pride can manifest itself as an inability to share even an emotional ownership of ideas or of the company's success with others. Pride can also cause the "Not Invented Here" syndrome within a top leader. It is the inebriant causing the delusion that the best solutions will only come from that leader him- or herself, or within his or her own company or industry. Pride also prevents one from admitting that he or she is in any way a contributor to any problem, and is one of the most common killers of great companies and inhibitors of growth.

Possible solutions: Most everyone has a few people in their lives with whom they place great trust and respect. Whether it is a mentor, family member (especially a parent), spouse, or spiritual authority, a trusted relationship might be the best connection to transform the heart of someone who is blinded with pride. Investors and other stakeholders who may have enough rapport with the leader could also be a possible door to the intervention. The bottom line is this: any intervention should involve clear, incontrovertible facts and multiple examples of the leader's pride. These truths and examples will illustrate how the leader's pride gets in the way of not just serving the customers' interests, but how it also hinders the company's growth, profitability, and even the leader's own wealth.

2. Abusive Relationships

Abuse often occurs through inappropriate relationships that may or may not be with consenting subordinates. The distrust and rancor resulting from such actions can ripple down from the president of the company all the way to the average employee.

Another example of abuse is displaying behaviors intended to demean and control others. This manifests itself in a lack of respect for a certain facet of the company, level of skill or talent, personality type, communication style, or, worse, a person's background, origin, or personal beliefs.

Possible solutions: Many of these abuse issues could be directed through human resources if there is a department or person handling such a role. Most people in our culture have enough sense of integrity that, if confronted one-on-one, they would admit that actions showing disrespect are wrong. Sexual relationships occurring at the top will require the proper higher authority, if there is one, to become involved. Also, managers who are prized and respected by the leader may be able to start a white-collar strike to show that they will not stand by and allow such abuse to continue.

3. Gossiping

Backbiting, backstabbing, badmouthing, and repeating any report that is not positive about others to those who have no responsibility in the matter is poison.

Even when a bad report is 100 percent factual, it is still gossip. Gossip has brought down many a reputation and company, both of which could have been repaired, and lives and jobs saved, had the gossiper followed a more healing path.

Possible solutions: Gossip is quite common yet I have often seen it successfully rooted out through the effective use of the Values Clarification and Reinforcement process outlined in Chapter 2. One former CEO of a Fortune 500 company would literally walk away from any conversation in which a bad report was being given. Word spread throughout the entire company (with tens of thousands of employees), and soon gossip became virtually absent and the company thrived. Later, a CEO of different colors came in, and not only did a different type of competition come into play, but the culture turned as well. Some said it was the lack of the "Good Report" culture that was the greater contributor to the company's demise. New leadership has started to bring the company back, but they had a long fall. The point is this: as a leader, regardless of your position, you can transform the culture of backstabbing by refusing to participate.

Another company I know has it written in their mission statement that their purpose was to improve the character of their employees and customers, *not* to make a profit. When they fired a highly productive older woman for gossip, the state Supreme Court held up the dismissal.

4. Greed

Greed can be displayed through unfair pay that is either too high or too low. Even now, corporate America is paying the price for undeserved bonuses and unusually high salaries, and I will not debate the right levels of such for a publicly held company, as that is a job for the stakeholders. In the vast majority of privately held companies, greed at the top often becomes obvious to the employees and growth is constrained as a result.

Possible solutions: The stakeholders of a privately held company are free to leave, and must make the effort to leave if pay is grossly unfair in any direction. Confronting the leader about the impact his or her greed is having would be a rousing wake-up call, especially if you mention the company's decline in morale, productivity, and profits.

5. Any of the Five Dysfunctions in the Principle of Authority

1. **Lack of a clear authority structure.** When the chain of command is not clearly defined, chaos, dysfunction, and frustration will ultimately ensue. This dysfunction is most frequently displayed in partnerships, whether 50/50 or some other equal split of authority. Eventually there will be decisions that can't be made, resulting in stress or arguments. Frustrations or jealousies due to unequal workloads or pay can also crop up in such partnership situations. **Possible solutions:** A clear titular authority, tiebreaker, or third-party advisory role can eliminate the dysfunction in decision-making and leadership. Whereas I prefer organic organizational charts that are in the shapes of circles or mind maps (because I have seen how they reduce the stuffiness of authority structures), there must be some chain of command and accountability. Despite

any distaste you may have for org charts, you need one, so consider the alternative shapes.

2. **Lack of respect for the chain of command.** When you have subordinates who disrespect the chain of command, they create conflict. The same goes for titular leaders who don't differentiate between the open door of communication and the proper channels of appeal. **Possible solution:** You may need to set a value or standard that reinforces the proper respect of the chain of command. But be careful not to squelch open communication.

3. **The inability to communicate up the ladder without fear of retribution** with legitimate appeals and a clear appeal process. One of the quickest ways to shut down communication and growth is to allow managers to get away with punishing subordinates who have made legitimate appeals or efforts to communicate appropriate matters up the chain of command. A company, like a government, does well to have a healthy process of appeal, without which bitterness and resentment will quickly grow and choke your employees' commitment and productivity. **Possible solutions:** There are two key principles here that, if put in place, can do much to improve communication, innovation, and growth, as well as reduce conflict and inappropriate behaviors. First, you as a leader must instill the value of trust in one's self (first by your own example) so that managers are not so overly protective of their own back that they become embittered by any confrontations from subordinates (which will inevitability come their way). Second, you must teach others to trust in the authority structure and process of management and appeals. Most people don't understand the appeal process in life or business, but it works much like our court system. There is always a higher authority that could be appealed.

But appeals must be made in a humble and respectful way. There are even Fortune 500 companies with appeal processes that allow employees to appeal all the way to the CEO. They are well managed, don't take that much of the CEO's time, and are transformational at building morale and trust in the leadership.

4. **The lack of checks and balances.** "Power corrupts, and absolute power corrupts absolutely." A titular leader with no checks and balances is bound to get into situations in which the lack thereof will stagnate growth in the team. Being a top leader requires you to constantly check your actions. Even if you feel your integrity is flawless, your subordinates might think otherwise. When setbacks, difficulties, and complications arise, find a solution to them quickly and efficiently, but always understand that, despite your belief that all has been resolved, in the hearts of those who feel wronged, opnions will often fester unresolved. These offenses will inevitably affect employees, and thus productivity, growth, and profit. You must instill checks and balances with your power to prevent this now and in the future when your succession plan takes hold. **Possible solutions:** I am amazed at how many boards have no concept of their authority and role. Board incompetence is mainly the fault of the titular leader. As such you must ensure that the best practices in board governance are regularly reviewed and agreed upon. If you lack a true and independent board, create one, or at least a board of advisors. Tell your team that you submit to the authority of the board in matters relevant to their authority, and that the board is a safety valve for the whole company.

5. **Megalomania and rebellion.** This can be displayed through the titular leader, whether it's a president that is an employee or an owner. Any leader who refuses to

submit to the higher authority of either a board of directors/advisors or the customer in appropriate matters will eventually endanger the existence of the organization. You can debate which areas may or may not be appropriate for the titular leader to submit to the input or directive of the customers or a board (even if he appointed it), but the main concern is whether or not that titular and seemingly autonomous leader is willing to submit to *anyone* on *anything*. The will to submit to correction is usually either there or not. Either the person tends to exhibit some signs of megalomania and general rebellion against other authorities, or that leader has some sense of true humility and thus is coachable and able to be a part of a turnaround when and if one is needed. There is no middle ground on this issue. The clear solution is that, as a leader, you must show that you truly are willing to submit to some higher authority on at least some issues. This topic segues into the sire of all leadership virtue: humility.

Humility, the Sire of All Virtue

There was a product manager at a large consumer products company who was forced to work with a haughty executive who was wont to wear his degrees on his sleeve. With his JD and MBA along with two undergraduate degrees he was quick to say, "I have a degree in..." and irritate the sense out of his coworkers. One day in reviewing a problem, he said to the product manager, "You know, I have a degree in this area, and...." The product manager interrupted and said, "Even thermometers have degrees, and you know where people stick thermometers." She was able to say it in a way that even he laughed. She had a gift with communication as well as a level of humility that this well-degreed executive did not.

There is no virtue in leadership as important to accelerated growth and turnaround as that of humility. Not so much because mistakes must be admitted but because the source of the solutions will come from without, not within. Your personal education and experience are probably not the key sources of the solutions that will be needed. The strength of the relationships you have and the process for synergizing those relationships, internal and external to your organization, will be the source of many ideas that will be the steps to your growth and turnaround.

A best practice to show and prove your humility is to have confidential blind-spot sessions. This is the simple but potentially painful practice of inviting your team, one by one, to meet with you to share your greatest blind spots that most hinder you and your company's growth. They are to point out your character missteps with specific examples, and, if they wish, discuss how it might have impacted others. When you as a leader can listen to, understand, acknowledge, and respond to the weaknesses that your subordinates bring to you in this setting, it will do more to bond your relationships and tap the full potential of your people than many a management tactic.

These confidential blind spot sessions are much more than the question in the Role Focus 12, "What are the things that my superior does that most hinder me?" Your people will bring up your character flaws and habits that may seem unrelated to your effectiveness—but they will bring them up for a reason. They will test you with smaller issues to see how you react, and if you take notes, confirm what you've heard, and not make excuses for the examples but acknowledge them and ask for help in keeping you accountable to better character in the future, you will see people transform before your eyes.

This one practice alone has saved bankrupt companies. Turning around a company is first about turning around the people, and the first turnaround is you!

←Lower Rate of Innovation

Higher Rate of Innovation→

The quality and strength of humility in an organization, especially as
exhibited by the top echelon, can have significant impact
on the potential of the organization to start a turnaround
as well as its ability to innovate.

Key Actions of a True Turnaround Leader

Uncover Relationship Opportunities

In larger organizations you may not be able to meet or call to
interview enough people in enough facets for the limited amount
of time you may have in a turnaround. Still, one-on-one, face-
to-face depth interviews will be your most effective means for
gleaning the insights you need. With time and travel constraints,
pack your calendar with phone interviews and consider using an
objective third party to flesh out additional interviews as needed.
If you are new to the organization, you don't have much time for

the assessment phase, but you also can't begin to pull certain triggers prematurely. There will probably be skeletons to uncover, and many people won't be overly excited to point them out.

Beyond assessing opportunities, more important is building relationships with those on your team whom you are there to serve. A top priority in a turnaround is to understand their personal objectives as clearly as you understand the organization's. In buy-outs and takeovers, the acquirers often parachute in and begin boasting of an aggressive vision for growth and the strategy, health, and successes of the acquiring company. These are not the first things that employees at a newly purchased company want to hear. The first questions they have are: "Do I have a job here? Are we relocating to another city? Will my compensation change? Will I keep the same healthcare benefits? Will I have the same parking spot? How am I valued by this new ownership?" Focus on your people first—their questions, needs, and objectives. Let them know you will help them get what they need and want and they will help you get what you need and want.

Change Symbols as Well as Your Actions

If you have been at your company for a while and have decided to take on the turnaround mindset, consider changing your title. For example, some leaders who succeeded at making the right impressions and turned things around changed their titles from CEO to: CIO, for Chief Innovation Officer; i-CEO, for interim CEO; CGO, for Chief Growth Officer; Adjunct COO or Adjunct VP of Operations for a part-time Operations Officer. On rare occasions I have heard people actually use the title Turnaround CEO or Turnaround VP.

Such changes could even be physical, such as locating a CEO's office in the middle of everything rather than at some far-flung corner office. Putting in glass walls around a leader's offices has also been a powerful symbol. I've seen leaders even take their door off its hinges to impress that the door is *literally* always open. Private rooms are probably available down the hall, so why not make the point? Drastic times call for...

Prioritize Action

Go through this book and rate the potential impact each suggestion could have in your company and prioritize ideas for action; this will help to build the beginnings of a plan that can help to grow your business. You also need the right people for all growth efforts to be successful—their buy-in and engagement. We suggest that you share copies of *Growth or Bust* and discuss your highlights from it with all members of your team and ask for their feedback on what they see to be the priorities for growth and top strategies to implement. This, combined with our resources available at **EchelonManagement.com** can help you to begin an ongoing process of optimizing growth.

Reach Out for Help

If you have been at your company for a while and know that the bar could be raised, consider consulting with a third party. Despite the fact that you know your business and may have decades of successful experience at growing business, a third-party consultant focused on growth may have faced the same problems 100 times to your 10. And when an engagement is positioned properly on the right objectives, just one profitable idea or new direction or strategy can make it worth it.

In Closing

Buy copies of this book for everyone on your team. Whether time is of the essence or not, consider assigning sections of the book and splitting up chapters. Then review, follow up, and assign tasks to appropriate teams.

One of the most powerful steps a CEO can take in using the principles of this book is to join a CEO round table echelon and/or introduce this book as a study guide for the group to discuss over time. Discuss what has been implemented with success and how ideas were implemented, as well as new ideas this book and the echeloning process has spawned. Call us if you need help in finding such a study group.

Also consider joining a virtual CEO roundtable where you can learn of and share more growth strategies that are working for companies just like yours. Go to *www.GrowthorBust.com* for more information.

I am a servant to the growth of business, jobs, and the economy. If my team or I can be of help to you, let us know. Echelon Management can serve your team at several levels. When time and budget are tight we can serve on small-scale projects and services like speeches to kick off the turnaround and overview concepts needed, or online or direct one-on-one phone coaching and support. On a middle scale, we can conduct depth interviews with key growth account customers. In larger-scale relationships we can be a part of facilitating quarterly strategic growth planning and other services, and in a full-scale engagement we can provide interim presidents, CEOs, VPs of sales, and turnaround teams.

Contact us at:

MarkFaust@EM1990.com

www.echelonmanagement.com

513-621-8000

The Call of the Leader

Whether you are in a struggle for your company's life or you just want to accelerate the growth of an already very successful company, you have a responsibility to the families that depend on your company. The most important customer might not be the one paying the bills or even the employees, but the children, the extended family, and the community that depends on your company—that depend on you to focus on facilitating innovation and growth.

Truly, it is growth or bust; their lives depend on it.

Carpe diem.

Index